DEAD RECKONINGS

A Review of Horror Literature
Edited by June M. Pulliam and Tony Fonseca
Kaci McClure, Editorial Assistant
Nos. 19/20 (Fall 2016)

Once upon a Midnight Dreary

Leigh Blackmore

ANN K. SCHWADER. *Dark Energies*. Sydney, Australia: P'rea Press, 2015. 110 pp. ISBN 9780994390103. AA $25; US $22; UK £14 tpb. [*Note:* A limited number of hc copies in pictorial boards were issued. Inquire of the publisher, DannyL58@hotmail.com.]

In her new collection *Dark Energies,* Ann K. Schwader, long one of our foremost poets of the weird and the speculative, demonstrates her versatility with form as well as with subject matter. Her verse ranges from homage to giants in the weird field (Clark Ashton Smith, Robert W. Chambers, H. P. Lovecraft) to poems imbued with her love of ancient civilizations to poignant and philosophical meditations on various states of being. Schwader excels at evoking with deft precision the dark energies that permeate the universe, including the myths and legends of earth's hidden corners.

A good example of one of Schwader's shorter poems is "Gone to Ground," which reads:

> There is no turning from the hounds of Time,
> No victory. In going swift to ground
> & burrowing through leaf-mold streaked with slime,
> There is no turning. From the hounds of Time
> A baying rises, signifying crime
> & punishment made one: your gravesite found,
> There is no turning. From the hounds of Time,
> No victory in going swift to ground.

The permutations of the opening line throughout the poem signify the omnipresence of the metaphorical hounds of Time, while the lines that follow are cleverly punctuated to illustrate the subject's desperate ducking and weaving to avoid it. Schwader here demonstrates accomplished control over form as well as content in brief compass.

The collection also features longer poems, such as "The Night of Her Return" (after Poe's "Ligeia"). In this verse, consisting of five six-line stanzas, Schwader essentially retells Poe's tale of unlooked-for reincarnation beyond the grave. In the first stanza, she cleverly works in the words "arabesques" and "grotesques," to echo Poe's early collection of tales, *Tales of the Grotesque and Arabesque* (1840). She also weaves in touches of her own interests in history and archaeology, so that "Sarcophagi from Luxor's sacred sites / Transform the obscure angles of this room / With auguries of life eternal, rites / Assuring swift deliverance from the tomb." Cumulatively, the poem becomes not simply a reiteration of Poe's tale, but a tribute in verse to his opulent imagination. The six-sonnet sequence "Keziah" contains many features of Lovecraft's famous tale "The Dreams in the Witch House," including the Black Man, Brown Jenkin (the rat-sized human-headed creature), and what Schwader aptly refers to as "the calculus of fear." A particularly unusual and delicious rhyme is "persuasions and equations" in stanza five. One of the longest poems is "Fiesta of Our Lady," which in ten six-line stanzas evokes a different Lovecraft tale, "The Curse of Yig," with atmosphere aplenty.

Other poems offer much to be enjoyed. "The Winds of Sesqua Valley" may mark the first poetic tribute to the worlds of W. H. Pugmire's fiction. "A Maid Betray'd" is both deceptively simple and extremely blood-chilling. Schwader's love for ancient Egyptian lore and legend evinces itself once more in such poems as "The Ba-Curse," "Horizon of the Aten" (with its poignant tribute to the dead commoners who slaved in life for the Pharaoh), "Set Comes to Whitechapel," and "Eating Mummy" (which seems to refer to the myth of Ammit, Eater of the Dead). "Wolves of Mars" is an unusual take on the werewolf, and "Of Pluto, P4, and Paranoia" is an up-to-date take on the relegation of Pluto from planet to "dwarf planet," with an echo back to Lovecraft's Yuggoth. The vampire is subtly conjured in the lines of "Mardi Gras Postmortem."

There are prose-poems here too: "Alexandria Next Time" presents a futuristic take on archivists and the great library; "Blown Out" tells of a serial killer with his victims near the bayou; "Torn Out" remembers the homeless who shelter in libraries; and "Alien Machines" creates a lasting impression of mysterious extraterrestrials.

The richness of Schwader's vision, and her mature ability to present emotional content through the medium of fantastic verse, to "conjure a world in a few strokes," as Robert M. Price puts it in his afterword, makes this a desirable purchase for any devotee of weird poetry. The volume also contains a preface by S. T. Joshi, a five-page interview of Schwader by Charles Lovecraft ("Into That Darkness Peering"), and several evocative black-and-white interior illustrations by cover artist David Schembri. *Dark Energies* is a quality production that solidifies its author's stature amongst modern weird poets. If there is the odd note of unnecessarily gendered language in some of these verses (for example, "constrained no longer by the laws of man" from "Nahab" and "what waits below is older than Man's dream" from "Fiesta of Our Lady"), this will scarcely be noticed by most readers (more's the pity). However, this is mere carping, in view of the overall imaginative quality of the verse.

The volume was a nominee for Superior Achievement in a Poetry Collection in the Bram Stoker Awards for 2015. Schwader was a Bram Stoker finalist for her *Wild Hunt of the Stars* (Sam's Dot, 2010) and was a Rhysling Award winner the same year, as well as Poet Laureate for NecronomiCon Providence 2015. She has published several previous volumes of poetry and prose.

Life Is More Horrible Than Death

S. T. Joshi

JACQUELINE BAKER. *The Broken Hours: A Novel of H. P. Lovecraft*. New York: Talos Press, 2016. c. 2014. 296 pp. ISBN: 9781940456553. $24.99 hc.

The appearance of H. P. Lovecraft (1890–1937) as a character in fiction goes back a surprisingly long way. In a sense we could trace it to as early as 1921, when Edith Miniter, one of Lovecraft's colleagues in the amateur journalism movement, wrote an exquisite parody of his work, "Falco Ossifracus: By Mr. Goodguile," in which the central figure was a send-up both of Randolph Carter (in "The Statement of Randolph Carter") and of Lovecraft himself. In recent decades, such authors as Richard A. Lupoff (*Lovecraft's Book* [1985]), Peter Cannon (*Pulptime* [1984], *The Lovecraft*

Chronicles [2004]), and many others have tried their hand at depicting Lovecraft as the focal point of adventures both natural and supernatural. Even the eminent Lovecraft biographer S. T. Joshi has written a silly thing called *The Assaults of Chaos* (2013).

It is safe to say that most of these works are, in large part, good-natured *jeux d'esprit,* filled with all manner of winks to Lovecraft devotees, but being fundamentally unserious in theme and spirit. That is the last thing that can be said of award-winning Canadian novelist Jacqueline Baker's *The Broken Hours,* an extraordinarily poignant and moving narrative that envisions a Lovecraft weighed down by a lifetime of sorrows and disappointments, and who in turn casts a pall of melancholy on all those around him.

There are several ways one can review such a book. A literalist approach, from the perspective of the book's perceived accuracy in treating its main subject, would find a fair number of errors and deficiencies. The very premise of the book defies credulity. We are asked to believe that, in the spring of 1936, when Lovecraft was living with his aunt, Annie E. Phillips Gamwell, at 66 College Street in Providence, he hired a secretary to handle the typing of his manuscripts and correspondence while Annie was in the hospital (supposedly for a case of "grippe"—an old-fashioned term for the flu—but in reality for a mastectomy to stem her breast cancer). The idea that the impoverished Lovecraft, earning virtually nothing and facing the crippling medical bills necessitated by Annie's illness, could have afforded such an amanuensis would make any Lovecraftian laugh; and most devotees also know that, while Lovecraft did indeed develop a kind of phobia of the typewriter, he rarely typed (or had others type) his correspondence, most of which exists in thousands upon thousands of pages of tiny, spidery handwriting.

But there is no question that Baker knows all this, for this implausible premise is only the springboard to introduce the protagonist, one Arthor [*sic*] Crandle, a man of Irish ancestry from Fall River, Massachusetts, who is himself down on his luck. Crandle is married to a woman named Jane. They once had a daughter, Molly, who died as a child; and although Arthor sends money back to Jane, their marriage is clearly strained.

Arthor settles into an attic room (Baker is no doubt aware

that Lovecraft, when moving into 66 College Street in 1933, had taken the "upper flat" for himself and his aunt, and that it contained, as he wrote in a letter, "5 rooms besides bath & kitchenette nook on the main (2nd) floor, plus 2 attic storerooms—one of which is so attractive that I wish I could have it for an extra den!") and gets down to work. One of the first things he does is to type a new story that Lovecraft has written, about a chambermaid in a hotel "down on Benefit Street near the waterfront." (I'm not entirely sure there was ever any hotel on Benefit Street at the time, nor is the street particularly close to the waterfront.) In all frankness, the story as Arthor describes it doesn't sound notably Lovecraftian, but its effect upon him is profound:

> I could not help but wonder at the kind of imagination—the kind of man—who would not only read but write such, well, I scarcely knew what to call it. Horror, I supposed. But not quite that, either. There was something about the world he depicted, the coldness of it, the meaninglessness, which disturbed me. There was nothing of humanity in it. Nothing of goodness. Nothing of hope. There was something dreadful and empty at its heart and, therefore, I imagined, at the heart of its author.
>
> To be the creator of all that hopelessness—well, how could one live with oneself? Darkness, I knew too well, begat only darkness. One way or another.

Perhaps this is an exaggerated portrayal of the effect of Lovecraft's own writings upon sensitive readers. And yet, when one reads such sentences as this one from "The Call of Cthulhu" (quoted by Baker later on in her novel)—"I have looked upon all that the universe has to hold of horror, and even the skies of spring and the flowers of summer must ever afterward be poison to me"—perhaps Arthor's reaction is not so exaggerated after all.

One ray of sunshine in this otherwise dispiriting book is Flossie Kush, a young woman who has sublet the first-floor apartment at 66 College. She is an aspiring actress who, throughout the novel, engages in a kind of flirtatious dance with Arthor, even though she knows he is married. Arthor himself is strongly attracted to her, although he has begun his relationship by deceiving Flossie as to his very identity, portraying himself as his employer.

The more Arthor learns about Lovecraft, the more disturbed he is—to the point that he begins to think of him as a monster. Anticipating the howls of Lovecraft's posthumous partisans, Baker allows Arthor to have several enigmatic talks with Lovecraft in his darkened study, with the result being that Arthor takes a very different view of his employer. Lovecraft tells Arthor the sad tale of his life: his father, Winfield, stricken with "paralysis" (in fact, it was syphilis) and spending the last five years of his life in Butler Hospital for the Insane; his mother, Sarah Susan ("Susie"), ending up in that same institution twenty years later, dying there in 1921; and in general the lot of a man and writer who was hailed as a prodigy in youth but who, at least by his own reckoning, had amounted to little now that his life was flickering to a close. Arthur is deeply moved by Lovecraft's confession: "I had seen into the heart of a stranger—a monster—and found it filled with such familiar longing and disappointment and despair that it might have been my own. How alike we all are. How broken." Later, after being disgusted by some of the lurid stories by Lovecraft and others in *Weird Tales,* Arthor concludes with what could well be the overriding theme of the novel: "Life, in my experience, provides all we need of horror." Or, as Lovecraft wrote in a plot synopsis for a story he may or may not have written: "Life is more horrible than death."

There is a wispy thread of supernaturalism in *The Broken Hours*—the apparent ghost of a little girl whom Arthor and others see from time to time. At first Arthor wonders if it could the ghost of his own Molly, but then decides it cannot be. The revelation of the ghost's true identity is one of the many quietly terrifying—and plangent—moments in this work. Susie Lovecraft, although she has been dead for fifteen years when the novel opens, also becomes a strangely disturbing character, as Baker tries to make sense of how this woman could have told people that her own son had a "hideous face."

If any criticism is to be made of *The Broken Hours,* it is that its various incidents don't seem to hang together very well. There is an episode where Arthor finds a group of people gathered around a beach at Narragansett Bay, where a sixteen-foot tentacle—severed from some immense creature—has drifted ashore; but nothing is made of this. Nor is it clear why so much is made of a person named Helen, from whom Flossie sublet the apartment, and whose funeral Flossie later attends. Arthor's wife, Jane, vows to pay him a visit, but then never arrives.

But these events, even if they have no direct bearing on the central plot, all contribute to the profound and pervasive atmosphere of sadness that every page of the novel emphasizes. *The Broken Hours* does not depict Lovecraft as he was, but uses him as a metaphor for the grim tragedy of human life, a tragedy whose anguish can only be allayed—if, indeed, it is not augmented—by being captured as weird fiction. No reader can fail to be moved by the lapidary fluency of Baker's prose, by her loving portrayals of her troubled characters, and by the cumulative power of a narrative that can only end in horror and bitterness. It is a triumph in every way.

Rotten Tomatoes?
How about Rotten Reviews?

June Pulliam

MIKE FLANEGAN, dir. *Hush*. Intrepid Productions, 2016. Netflix. JORDAN GALLAND, dir. *Ava's Possessions*. ODD NY–Off Hollywood, 2015. Netflix.

As you may know, usually only the most profitable horror films make it to first-run theaters, but streaming services such as Netflix, Hulu, Screambox, and Shudder offer many other films that fans might not otherwise be able to view. That is the case with two recent horror films available on Netflix, Mike Flanagan's slasher film *Hush* and the comic horror film *Ava's Possessions,* directed by Jordan Galland. *Hush* had received high ratings on Netflix and was discussed enthusiastically on social media, while *Ava's Possessions* got only a mediocre Netflix user rating. My experience viewing these two films has taught me to ignore the Netflix viewer scores, as *Hush* is an overly generic, while *Ava's Possessions* was a fresh comic take on the possession narrative.

As of this writing, *Hush* has a 100% fresh rating on Rotten-tomatoes.com. One reviewer gushed that the film "upend[s] horror tropes . . . and make us wonder why we liked them in the first place." This makes we wonder if that reviewer knows anything about horror, as *Hush* just wallows in these tropes without making any substantial change to them. The only question in my mind at the end of the film is why I devoted approximately two hours of my life watching it. Perhaps *Hush*'s makers thought that they had created a fresh take on the genre because the woman menaced by the killer is deaf. Maddie (played by Flanagan's wife Kate Siegel) is a successful novelist living alone in an isolated rural house. After a scene in which she chats with her visiting neighbor and establishes for the audience just how her inability to hear makes her uniquely vulnerable, the masked killer (a nod to The Purge franchise, perhaps) shows up to terrorize her. (The film is also an obvious ripoff of *Wait until Dark* [1967], in which a blind Audrey Hepburn is slowly terrorized by a menacing Alan Arkin.)

Apparently Maddie has no curtains or blinds in the bottom half of her window-filled house, so the killer plays cat and mouse with her for about thirty minutes by appearing at different windows while brandishing a weapon to demonstrate to his would-be victim just how vulnerable she is. Being a Southerner, I was incredulous that a woman living alone in a rural area had no weapon to protect her. I kept thinking that she could have just hidden and shot him the moment he entered her home, but then the movie would be over in record time. Instead, Maddie cowers and hides long enough for the killer to rip out her landline and disable her Internet connection, and even sneak in to steal her cell phone. Maddie eventually sneaks outside to have the predictable showdown with the slasher after he murders an arriving male neighbor who sees the killer and dies trying to fight him off.

Then the movie ends. The killer is dead, Maddie is alive, and the viewer realizes that she has lost two hours of her life. *Hush*'s plot is that of pretty much every slasher film since *The Texas Chainsaw Massacre,* yet it is so starkly minimalist that we have no backstory for the characters, and they have no motivation beyond the killer's love of terrorizing and Maddie not wanting to die. That is just lackluster scriptwriting and lazy, perhaps even cynical, directing. There is no foreshadowing of details as there are in *The*

Texas Chainsaw Massacre, such as an ominous horoscope reading for one of the characters and the occasional radio broadcast in the background about senseless violent crimes committed in other places, reminding the viewer that the whole world has gone crazy. So anyone who would say that this film upends horror tropes hasn't seen very many good horror films.

Worse yet, *Hush* inaccurately represents deafness. When someone loses the use of one sense, the others become heightened; but in the film, Maddie seems to have only her sense of sight to guide her, and this sense is no better than anyone else's. Thus, the killer just appears on the other side of the glass to terrify Maddie—without her feeling the vibrations of his feet as they hit the deck outside of her house—and he can sneak into her dwelling to steal an item without her smelling his presence . . . the list could go on and on. I guess that writer/director Flanagan left out these elements, as they are not easy to represent on the screen and would have taken vision and hard work.

Ava's Possessions received only a 62% fresh rating on Rottentomatoes.com, but several reviewers liked it, including Rob Staeger of the *Village Voice,* who said that the film "begins where most demonic possession films end." Staeger's observation explains precisely why *Ava's Possessions* is worth seeing, as it is a witty observation on the genre. Most possession films, most famously *The Exorcist,* focus on a teen body that is invaded by demons, something that represents the societal fear of feminine sexuality in general. These films end when the teen girl in question is appropriately subdued after the demons are evicted from her flesh—and the world is safe for patriarchy once more. *Ava's Possessions* opens as the titular character is tied to a bed and writhing as she is exorcised by a priest. After the demon has been driven from her, Ava learns that she has been possessed for a month: during this time, she has assaulted people, damaged property, had sex with strangers in public, and taken various illegal narcotics; moreover, she now faces criminal charges for these activities. So Ava is in a situation similar to that of an alcoholic or a drug addict who has bottomed out and must now make amends to people that she has harmed while under the influence.

In order to avoid going to jail for her actions, Ava is compelled to join Spirit Possession Anonymous, an organization like

Alcoholics Anonymous or Narcotics Anonymous, which requires participants to work a twelve-step program. It develops that the program is riddled with sexism in that it does not acknowledge that male and female members have different experiences that might not respond to SPA's one-size-fits-all treatment. SPA members are compelled to re-experience their possession in the safe space of the group until they are able to throw off the demons unassisted. However, SPA does not acknowledge a truth known to many of the female members: that demonic possession, like the spirit possession of Spiritualist mediums, allows them to articulate desires that are antithetical to stereotypical femininity and, in fact, puts them in touch with anger and the ability to do violence that can save their lives. Ava befriends a woman in the group who longs to be possessed again, as the presence of the demon in her body gave her abilities not available to her while "sober"—for example, her supernatural strength that came with her demonic possession allowed her to beat up the would-be rapist of a friend.

As Ava searches for the people she harmed in order to make amends, she begins to piece together what she did while under the influence of the demon, and this story is very different from the one of senseless sex and drunkenness told to her by her family and attorney. While Ava may have been promiscuous and intoxicated while possessed, she also defended herself against a would-be killer, and she must invite this demon in again to have the strength to fight off another attack. Overall, I am genuinely shocked by the negative reviews that I have seen of this film, as I was pleased by the conflation of gender and possession with the sexism inherent in many twelve-step fellowships. *Ava's Possessions* also boasts a strong cast, including several actors who have appeared in Netflix series, such as Carol Kane from *The Unbreakable Kimmy Schmidt* and Alysia Reiner and Deborah Rush from *Orange Is the New Black*. If nothing else, the supporting performances of these excellent veteran character actresses makes *Ava's Possessions* worth watching.

A Geriatric Anti-Hero, Splatstick, and Retro Rock

Chris Dallis

CRAIG DiGREGORIO, BRUCE CAMPBELL, IVAN RAIMI, SAM RAIMI, and ROB TAPERT, executive producers. *Ash vs. Evil Dead.* Renaissance Pictures-Starz, 2015–16.

> "When evil shows up, it blows up."
> Ash Williams, *Ash vs. Evil Dead*, Episode 4 ("Brujo")

If you grew up in the 1980s and were a horror film fan, there is a good chance that no movie scared the hell out of you more than the first *Evil Dead* film in 1981. I can still remember seeing it with my best friend at the time in a local theater. I read about this gruesome horror film in *Fangoria,* where no less than Stephen King himself gave it a resounding endorsement, which meant that any self-respecting genre fan had to see it as soon as possible. My best friend's parents were much more liberal than my own, so a shady deal was quickly struck: they would take us to the film and then pick us up immediately after the showing, even though it was a school night, a time during the week when these types of cinematic excursions were typically not allowed due to important homework responsibilities. Nevertheless, inexplicably, some kind of dubious deal was struck—and we were allowed to go see the film. We both had no idea just how rattled we were going to be by this cinematic ordeal, or how it would lead to one of the most celebrated horror franchises of our misspent youths.

After the film, I had to walk home from my friend's house, and I was so terrified that I sprinted the entire way in a mad panic, convinced of the likelihood that a host of possessed evil dead might tear me apart and then swallow my soul. I recalling telling my peers at the bus stop the next morning about the unease I experienced during the film, and everyone was aghast at the sights and sounds I encountered *and* was skeptical that their parents would actually take them to see such a wholesale bloodbath. Later, when the sequels—*Evil Dead II* (1987) and *Army of Darkness*

(1992)—came out, the franchise traded in fright for what eventually became known to genre fans as "splatstick," an entertaining combination of slapstick comedy and cartoonish splatter effects. The apotheosis of splatstick was achieved in the early cult films of Peter Jackson, *Bad Taste* (1987) and *Dead Alive* (1992), but it was certainly Sam Raimi's *Evil Dead II* that laid the foundational inspiration for the budding New Zealand director's now-legendary and outlandish combination of gore and guffaws.

The *Evil Dead* franchise's hero, Ash Williams, also changed as the tone of the sequels transmogrified from terror to mirth: he went from a lantern-jawed and straight-faced hero in the first film to being a wiseass jerk anti-hero by the third film. However, Bruce Campbell's brilliant and charismatic performance as Ash Williams effortlessly carried fans through the proceedings and made things all the more fun in the second and third films, even if events became considerably less chilling than in the original franchise entry.

In 2013, when Sony Pictures remade the original *Evil Dead,* many fans liked the fact that the franchise now returned to a more serious tone, but just as many called the film out for its overuse of Japanese horror film tropes and CGI, and alas, for its lack of an Ash Williams. Consciously or unconsciously, it seems that the recent *Ash vs. Evil Dead* series has answered the prayers of all the hardcore fans who wanted to see the original Ash Williams and all the splatsticky fun he came to represent. The ten-episode Starz series starts in Ash's trailer in episode one, and then ends up, by the eighth segment, back at the creepy cabin in the woods that set the whole Evil Dead phenomenon in motion so many years ago. One of the highlights of the first episode is an opening flash-cut montage that references the now-famous one found in *Evil Dead II,* where Ash straps himself into weaponry for a climatic showdown with the evil possessed and ends up deadpanning the absurdist word "groovy" into the camera.

In comedic inversion, the montage in *Ash vs. Evil Dead* reveals Williams to be strapping himself into a compression garment to hide his middle-aged gut. He dances about like a fool, grabs some condoms, and then dashes out to a dive bar to see if he can score some recreational love. At the bar, he lies to a mark about his fake hand and plies her with drinks. During their tryst in the

bathroom, his one-night stand turns into a deadite. Rattled by this most unwelcome occurrence during sex, Ash returns to his trailer confused and grabs his copy of the *Necronomicon* for a possible explanation, only to discover a curious bag of weed inside it. It is then revealed in a flashback that Ash, when high, tried to impress a previous one-night hookup he brought to his trailer by reading her some "poetry" from the *Necronomicon,* hence loosing evil, once again, back into our world.

In a parallel story line, a pair of Michigan state cops are seen investigating a report that a woman was heard screaming for her life. The woman turns out to be the poetry enthusiast from Ash's flashback. Now possessed by evil, she and the State Police do bloody supernatural battle, which leads one officer, Amanda, to become embroiled in the quest to investigate. Amanda's exchange with the girl ends up leading to the death of her partner, so her quest for answers becomes personal.

Meanwhile, Ash digs out the business card of a bookseller and translator of obscure texts to help him reverse the damage he resurrected by reading unhallowed passages while stoned. He arrives at his lame job as a retail salesman, where viewers are introduced to the two fellow deadite fighters, Pablo and Kelly, who will aid him in his quest to defeat the evil dead once again. This episode also introduces the character Ruby, a mysterious person who, like state cop Amanda, is also looking for Ash to get to the bottom of the supernatural shenanigans that are now plaguing the state of Michigan. While working his retail job, Pablo helps Ash defeat a possessed doll in the business's warehouse, and then Pablo discloses that his uncle is a shaman who told him that a mythical man would rise up and stand against the world's evil. Pablo relates that he believes Ash may be this hero, but Ash has plans to just try and outrun the horror he has spawned. "You can't outrun evil, Ash," Pablo warns, but Ash returns "Watch me!"

Later, however, as Ash plans to run away, a blood-littered deadite attack unfolds at his trailer. True to form, Ash's trusty chainsaw and shotgun end up saving him, Kelly, and Pablo. Stunned that this wholesale jerk Ash turns out to be hero capable of defeating an unholy onslaught, Kelly and Pablo wonder what it feels like for the famous slayer of demons to be back in action again. His response? You guessed it: "Groovy."

Punctuating this in-joke, the song "The Journey to the Center of the Mind," by Amboy Dukes, mixes up for the credit sequence. The rest of the nine segments in this brilliant series are littered with everything a fan of the original trilogy would expect: lots of supernatural shaky cam footage, lots of delightful and gratuitous gore, and lots and lots of wisecracks and politically incorrect smart-assery from Ash Williams. The show is also graced by a mind-blowing soundtrack of retro rock classics that somehow flawlessly complements the action and characters. I find it hard to fathom that any fans of the original films would not be utterly thrilled about everything this series has to offer—hilarity, excitement, great storytelling, and Bruce Campbell, scene stealing at every conceivable turn. The series will be returning for another season, so I would strongly suggest that all fans of quality horror comedy entertainment not pass this one over.

Famous Men of Filmland

Tony Fonseca

JASON V and SUNNI K BROCK, director/producers. *Charles Beaumont: The Short Life of Twilight Zone's Magic Man*. JaSunni Productions, 2010. 88 min. ASIN: B004HKIVCS. DVD $18.95. JASON V and SUNNI K BROCK, director/producers. *The Ackermonster Chronicles,* 2013. 105 min. ASIN: B00AW27N10. DVD $22.95.

If there is one sign of an excellent biographical documentary film, it is that the producer and director are absolutely head over heels in love with their subject matter. It is not difficult to tell when this happens. For one thing, visuals makes it very clear how the creative staff behind a documentary biopic feel—the interviewers themselves are rarely on camera, as all visuals are devoted to the subject, the subject and other interviewees are allowed to interview in a comfortable place of their own choosing (you could say they are made to feel at home), and the interviewees are allowed free rein to explore their thoughts, rather than being constantly barraged with questions. Viewers of JaSunni Productions' *Charles Beaumont: The Short Life of Twilight Zone's Magic Man* and *The Ackermonster Chronicles* do not have to watch for very long before they realize that the creative talent behind the two films, Jason V and Sunni K Brock, love their subject matter so much they simultaneously allow the story to unfold via interviews while re-creating that story into an artistic whole—a work of art—worthy of the story being told. Viewers will also count themselves fortunate that JaSunni learns from its mistakes as it goes: problems in sound that slightly mar their 2010 biopic on Charles Beaumont are nowhere present on their 2013 study of Forrest J Ackerman.

But first to the obvious: no matter what technical mastery a production team exhibits in a documentary, the end product is a failure if the subject matter is either unengaging or is approached in a lackluster way. The Brocks win over the viewer immediately with their choices of subject matter. Charles Beaumont is arguably the least studied of the brilliant core team of *Twilight Zone* screenwriters—the others being Rod Serling, Richard Matheson, and George Clayton Johnson—despite the acknowledgment among his peers (including the aforementioned venerable trio of screenwriters) that he was the most talented of the group. *Charles Beaumont: The Short Life of Twilight Zone's Magic Man* makes up for this injustice (and then some) by allowing a who's who of science fiction and weird fiction authors to talk about their interactions with Beaumont, who died in 1967 from a rare form of Alzheimer's and Pick's at the age of thirty-eight. Interviewees include luminaries Forrest J Ackerman, Ray Bradbury, Harlan Ellison, George Clayton Johnson, Richard Matheson, William F. Nolan, Roger Corman, and William Shatner; as well as people who knew Beaumont personally and current historians, authors, and literary critics, John and Wilma Tomerlin, Frank M. Robinson, Dennis Etchison, John Shirley, Marc Scott Zicree, Roger Anker, Norman Corwin, and S. T. Joshi; and even Beaumont's son Christopher. The interviews are edited so seamlessly that the diverse voices eventually meld into one tragic story of a man who lived a lifetime in less than forty years.

The interviews are both engaging and insightful, as they bring together the aforementioned benchmark writers and actors, who talk about not just Beaumont as writer, but Beaumont as a larger-than-life personality, revealing that he was a man driven by passion for life. Despite his constant debilitating headaches (near the end of the documentary it is revealed that he had all the signs of aluminum poisoning from the Bromo-Seltzer he drank daily), he showed a flair for living: he would crash parties of dignitaries and find himself invited to some of the most exclusive parties, both in Hollywood and throughout the United States; he bought stock cars and raced them whenever he had the opportunity; he placed stories in *Playboy* regularly; he even wrote and acted alongside William Shatner in a Roger Corman movie (*The Intruder,* 1962). The documentary also features researcher Marc Scott Zicree (*The Twilight Zone Companion,* 1992), who offers a historical perspective. Without a doubt, this JaSunni film is a must-see (and must-own) for all fans of speculative fiction, whether they be affiliated with science fiction, horror, or fantasy. For *Twilight Zone* fans, it is a rare opportunity to watch two of the four great script writers of that series tells stories about one of their colleagues. It is also an opportunity to see in interview legendary writers who have passed on since 2010. As mentioned, the only knock against this production is that it smacks of early (perhaps even first) film production values. Aside from some of the aforementioned sound issues (which occur in more than one interview), at times problems with video occur as well that make the production seem amateurish—although some of the "accidents" are charming, such as when one interviewee's cat decides to video-bomb the interview.

Without losing any of the charm, *The Ackermonster Chronicles* shows a vast improvement in production technique. At times moving backgrounds (usually behind Forrest J Ackerman, who does the bulk of the interview in what is obviously his favorite lounge chair) come across as kitschy, but Ackerman was all about kitsch, so even over-the-top visuals work well. Moreover, they never detract from Ackerman himself, who comes across as one of the truly brilliant minds of the genre (he shows an astounding memory for details, for example). To me, the documentary should get the highest praise bestowed upon an artifact of its ilk—it actually makes the viewer wish he/she were in the room during the interview, or at least it makes the viewer want to share a table and a pitcher of beer with Ackerman (who died in 2008). The best way to describe the Ackerman whom JaSunni Productions reveals is to quote the Amazon description of the video: "Freaks! Mutants! A world gone mad! Nudism. Esperanto. King Kong. 'Sci-Fi.' What do all these things have in common? Simple: Forrest J Ackerman." The description goes on to state that Ackerman

> was an agent, a notorious, serial bit player, and an honorary lesbian. Known the world over as "Uncle Forry," "EEEE," "4SJ," "Dr. Acula," and numerous other pseudonyms (a few none too kind), Mr. Ackerman was perhaps best known as the original editor of *Famous Monsters of Filmland* magazine, the creator of Vampirella, and all-around mega-fan!

As "out there" as the description seems, it is accurate. Ackerman was not only an agent; he was THE agent. His clients included Charles Beaumont, A. E. Van Vogt, William F. Nolan, Curt Siodmak, and L. Ron Hubbard—and they knew that he worked hard for them. Some of Ackerman's best interview stories involve some of the tricks he would pull to get a writer published, as well as his all-too-enthusiastic methods of letting them know they had sold stories. If you were a science fiction luminary and he wasn't your agent, he was your friend (and probably biggest fan). He befriended Ray Harryhausen, Ray Bradbury, Vincent Price, and John Landis. He got Price's final autograph. In short, he was the driving force behind fantasy and science fiction. He even turned his home into a museum (The AckerMansion) and gave free tours to anyone who was interested in seeing his collection.

As in the Charles Beaumont biopic documentary, here again Jason V Brock allows his interview subject to be himself, to control the interview in such a way that it comes across as just a pleasant conversation between two friends or colleagues who want to reminisce and maybe do a little social commentary in the meantime. In addition to Ackerman, interviewees include Ray Bradbury, Richard Matheson, John Landis, Joe Dante, William F. Nolan, Dan O'Bannon, W. H. Pugmire, Ray Harryhausen, Greg Bear, John and Wilma Tomerlin, Christopher Beaumont, Marc Scott Zicree, George Clayton Johnson, and David J. Skal. Viewers who grew up reading *Famous Monsters of Filmland* or watching horror films in the 1950s and 1960s will find much to enjoy in this documentary, which is filled with one fascinating interview after another, all interspersed around Ackerman's fascinating reminiscences of Hollywood.

Of Old Ones and Zombies

Richard Bleiler

CHARLES BLACK. *Black Ceremonies*. Lancashire, UK: Parallel Universe Publications, 2015. 168 pp. ISBN: 9780957453555. £8.99 tpb.
PHIL SMITH. *The Footbook of Zombie Walking*. Axminster, UK: Triarchy Press, 2015. 149 pp. ISBN: 9781909470873. £13.00 tpb.

Charles Black's *Black Ceremonies* and Phil Smith's *The Footbook of Zombie Walking* are both fairly slim, with uninspiring, even amateurish cover artwork. While they share a crucial ideational linkage, they differ greatly: one is a collection of stories and the other an odd blend of literary theory, philosophy, and cinema.

Black collects thirteen stories, eight of which were published previously, generally in small-press venues. A number of the thirteen make use of aspects of the Cthulhu Mythos, both through the dropping of names and through the overt use of subject matter. In no case, however, do any of the stories rise above the flat and mediocre: they are uniformly amateurish, with all the unfortunate implications that can be inferred from that term. First, and sadly, what seems to be entirely too many of the stories appear to be set in a world that is unaware of the existence of women. They consist of conversations between men, with little evidence given to indicate that any of the speakers have ever even seen a woman, much less talked with her. Next, the stories do occasionally posit intriguing and even amusing ideas, as in "Face to Face," "The Revelations of Dr. Maitland," and "A Bit Tasty," but the first lacks suspense, telling rather than showing; and the latter two are weak and flat, completely dependent on their closing lines to make their points, and they thus make one realize what a clever stylist could have built to and accomplished.

In all the stories, the dialogue is unconvincing, the characterizations are uninspiring, the developments fail to cohere, and the climaxes fail to satisfy. The majority of the stories are set in England, weakly and unconvincingly rendered although that is apparently Black's residence; but when Black attempts a new location, as in the spaghetti-western-inspired "A Fistful of Vengeance," the results are sadly risible, almost a textbook example of why even inspirations need editing. Even at a mere thirteen pages, the story needs compressing, and a firm editorial presence might have convinced Black that frontier American hotels did not possess "Do Not Disturb" signs. If one wants contemporary male writers of stories of the Cthulhu Mythos, one can turn elsewhere—Ramsey Campbell, Thomas Ligotti, and Darrell Schweitzer all do consistently solid work. *Black Ceremonies* is not a necessary read.

The same cannot be said about *The Footbook of Zombie Walking,* though whether it is necessary or not depends on how philosophically inclined and well-informed the putative reader happens to be. Early in the volume, Smith states that *Footbook* is "a guidebook for walking the world with alternative manners." What it is, really, is a series of chapters that discuss aspects of zombies in their various depictions, with questions and suggestions for the readers interspersed. If one is attuned to this sort of thing, such passages as this—"Shinji Mikami, the originator of the 'Resident Evil' computer game dubbed the sub-genre 'Survival Horror.' As Slavoj Žižek has it, 'the obscene immortality of the 'living dead' which, after every annihilation, recompose themselves and clumsily go on . . . an uncanny urge to repeat painful past experiences that seems to outgrow the natural limitations of the organism affected by it and to insist even beyond the organism's death" (ellipsis in the original)—will stimulate thought. If one is not so attuned, other texts that discuss the philosophies surrounding zombies and the living dead are certainly available. Furthermore, Smith has made a number of assumptions in his writings about the meanings of space and zombies that can and should be challenged, and doing so is sometimes very rewarding.

Nevertheless, it must be emphasized that these comments are not meant to dismiss or disparage *Footbook,* for it offers much that can be savored and enjoyed. Smith is well-informed and clearly loves his subject, and his exercises and suggestions can be stimulating. In addition, many of Smith's theoretical zombie-centric discussions are quite lively. At the same time, *Footbook* has some irksome deficiencies, and the worst may be Smith's bibliography, which is grossly incomplete, listing only a selection of his references and none of the many motion pictures to which he makes frequent allusions. Thus, although numerous authors, auteurs, and their works are discussed, few are so much as listed; the curious reader who wishes to follow the *Footbook* by examining Smith's inspirations will need to turn to the Internet Movie Database (www.imdb.com) or Wikipedia for complete citations. In addition, *Footbook* has no index.

The beginning of this review stated that the two books, though very dissimilar, shared an ideational linkage. It is this—both are derivational works. That works are derivational does not mean they are inherently deficient or inadequate; rather, it means that the writers are dependent upon their audiences' possessing a knowledge of and an interest in genre material and that the work in question makes use of this material to appeal to these audiences. In the case of *Black Ceremonies,* Black consistently fails to do justice to his material, though it is quite possible that he may improve: he may recognize that to write a successful Mythos story one must do more than recycle. In the case of *Footbook,* Smith takes what already exists and does something very clever with it, creating an original amalgamation. I wish him additional success as well as the recognition that his volumes would benefit by the addition of those traditional appurtenances of scholarship, complete bibliographies and full indexing.

Not for the Faint of Heart

Greg Gbur

LIVIA LLEWELLYN. *Furnace.* Petaluma, CA: Word Horde, 2016, 193 pp. ISBN: 9781939905178. $13.50 tpb.

Livia Llewellyn's fiction is not for the faint of heart, or the casual reader of horror looking for a touch of weird reading before bed. Llewellyn writes about some of the darkest aspects of human nature, associated with some of the most taboo topics in society. Her stories are often intensely sexual and commonly include not only lust and temptation but sexual assault, abuse, and violence. These observations are not intended as a criticism. Llewellyn's writing is intense, powerful, and unforgiving. This is aptly demonstrated in her most recent collection, *Furnace*. The slender volume contains thirteen stories, written mostly between 2010 and 2014, with one earlier story from 2007.

Furnace is only her second collection, after *Engines of Desire: Tales of Love & Other Horrors* (2011). Nonetheless, her short fiction has appeared in many publications since 2005 and is highly acclaimed: *Engines of Desire* was nominated for the Shirley Jackson Award for Best Single-Author Collection. I am tempted to say that her stories feel like literary contradictions: poetic and elegant while simultaneously incredibly horrific. Many of them have a dream, or should I say nightmare, quality to them, while others take the form of conventional narrative.

The first story of the collection, "Panopticon," is a dreamlike tale set in the factory district on the edge of a strange city named Obsidia, with a population of seemingly anonymous residents. The unnamed protagonist of the story travels, first on subway and then on foot, to an abandoned factory building, drawn there by an irresistible impulse. What she finds at the end of her journey is an impossible combination of ecstasy and agony, and it lasts forever. In the exceedingly uncomfortable story "Stabilimentum," Thalia struggles to get used to her new city apartment, thirty floors up. Though she thought she would like being so far away from the streets, she now finds the presence of so many neighbors, pressing against her own space, distressing. Things are made even worse when she ends up with a new neighbor: a bloated black spider in the upper corner of her bath. She hastily dispatches the intruder, but another appears. And another. In the face of growing horror, Thalia must come to terms with what she truly desires.

A seemingly innocent family reunion on the Washington coast is found to be something much darker in "The Last, Clean, Bright Summer." Through the journal of a teenager, Hailie, we are exposed to a coming-of-age story of a particularly nasty sort, as an ancient ritual necessary for humanity's survival is enacted.

Set in the final years of the eighteenth century, "Cinereous" follows Olympe, a Parisian woman who has found employment in a sadistic scientific research complex. She takes her job seriously and does it with pride, collecting the remains of the butchered test subjects. But she will learn that very little separates the studier and the studied. In "In the Court of King Cupessacae, 1982," thrill-seeking Severin ignores the warnings of her not-quite-human lover Knox and crashes an extremely exclusive house party in Bellingham. Rather than being turned away, she is welcomed—though the price of admission, and that of seeing the King, is more than she can imagine.

My impression, from viewing the collection in its entirety, is that Llewellyn's stories explore the destructive nature of relationships, primarily but not exclusively through the sexual. In "It Feels Better Biting Down," obsessively close twin sisters find a way to make their unity a literal one. In "Allochthon," the stagnant relationship of a long-married couple becomes even supernaturally repetitive, to the breaking point. In the only story obviously based on the work of another, "Yours Is the Right to Begin," the undead wives of *Dracula* (1897) reach out to Mina Harkness in dreams to explain what is expected of her when she joins the fold. In "And Love Shall Have No Dominion," a passing encounter links a supernatural being of lust with an innocent woman; the obsession of the being inevitably leads to death, pain, and destruction. The final story of the collection, "The Unattainable," is a more conventional, non-supernatural erotic tale, in which an aging and lonely woman meets her sexual match in a fierce and apparently untamable man.

What is most impressive here is that there is not a wasted story in the collection: all possess a passion and intensity that can be simultaneously hard to read and impossible to put down. As already noted, this collection is not for everyone, due to the highly intense and possibly triggering subject matter. For those willing to go deeper and darker than most, however, Livia Llewellyn's *Furnace* is a compelling and fascinating read.

The Killer and the Killed

June Pulliam

MICHAEL ARONOVITZ. *Phantom Effect*. New York: Night Shade Books, 2016. 292 pp. ISBN 9781597808460. $15.99 tpb.

The cover and title of Michael Aronovitz's newest novel *Phantom Effect* tell you little about what awaits you inside, which is so much more than just another serial killer novel about a crazed loner who has "issues with women." Jonathan Deseronto embodies every stereotype of the serial killer. His extreme masculine sense of self, expressed through his violence toward women, is the result of an absent father and a literally castrating mother. The adult Deseronto is "six foot five" with a "granite jaw and deep carved lines around [his] mouth like judgments." He works for other men doing what is typical men's work—fixing "gas compressors, slab saws, and power tools"—and he keeps "dirty magazines under [his] workbench" and wears "a blue canvas monkey suit with [his] name stitched in an oval on [his] chest." Because he does not have a working set of testicles, he believes that the only way he can be intimate with a woman is to kill her, something that has is preternaturally good at, in keeping with other fictional serial killers. Afterwards, Deseronto cuts his victims' bodies into seventeen parts, which he buries in a shallow grave. Deseronto is never caught, never even a suspect in the disappearance of his victims, since like the fictional Dexter Morgan, he is meticulous about cleaning up his carnage; but in spite of his imposing height, he is able to blend into his surroundings so that he is never noticed. Deseronto's last victim, Marissa Madison, is the yin to his yang. Marissa embodies all the stereotypes of hegemonic femininity—both beautiful and in possession of such a high degree of intuition that she knows people's deepest secrets before they do. Predictably, Madison can best use this intuition to help others more than herself—she is a sort of psychic helpmate. So although she senses Deseronto tracking her, she is unable to prevent him from killing her.

Yet although Aronovitz's characters are rooted in well-known character types, *Phantom Effect* is not a formulaic work of maniac fiction, but instead, a serious and character-driven examination of a genre that is based on extremes of gender. Both the killer and the victim are Others. Deseronto is that kid we all went to school with, the student whose peers sensed that there was something "off" about him. Deseronto is rather like the young Jeffrey Dahmer in this regard: while his antisocial behavior might win him the admiration of other male classmates who were amused by his ability to disrupt school with pranks while not getting caught, he was too unsettling for them to actually befriend. Deseronto, like young Dahmer, is smart but does poorly in school because he is not interested in the subject matter and wrestling with too many demons of his own to care about his future. Deseronto is similar to the kid who we predicted would grow up doing manual labor to support his interests in crime and violence before he eventually landed in jail. Marissa too is a sort of Other among her peers, but for different reasons. She is the privileged, pampered girl whose beauty and intuition unnerve everyone, so her peers are loath to get too close to her as well. Yet in Aronovitz's hands, Madison and Deseronto are not wooden stereotypes, but elemental forces who are destined to meet for their bloody encounter in which the two extremes collide.

While Deseronto may have killed Madison, he has not silenced her, and he cannot even control her body, which he has sliced into seventeen pieces and put into a trash bag in the trunk of his car. Instead, the dismembered Madison stitches herself back together with some fishing wire she finds in Deseronto's trunk and emerges from this space to hijack his consciousness and, like a dark version of the angel in *It's a Wonderful Life,* forces him to rifle through his memories, but for the purpose of confronting his own vulnerabilities. The novel is related through multiple perspectives—Deseronto's first-person perspective, in which he justifies his crimes to himself and congratulates himself on his own cleverness; Madison's perspective, through which we come to sympathize with her as well as feel dread as she relates her last moments before her murder; and an omniscient perspective through which we see what the characters cannot. Deseronto and Madison are both subjects and objects of this discourse. For the female Madison, this dual perspective is familiar, as women are habituated to view themselves as objects of an overarching Male Gaze in which they are potentially on display as an object of desire. But this dual perspective is unsettling for the male Deseronto, who is the violent extremity of this gaze. For him, it is worse to experience himself on the other end of this gaze, to see himself as others see him, and even to see what he has hidden from himself, than it is to be captured and imprisoned for his crimes.

Aronovitz is like Thomas Harris in how his serial killer narrative is about so much more than merely a voyeuristic account of a crazed young loner murdering women. Rather, the novel invites us to consider how the killer is a creation of patriarchy who polices the outer limits of femininity in order to subordinate women. While his extra-legal actions are officially disavowed by society, they also serve as a warning to women who would step too far from their assigned gender roles. In this way, Aronovitz's fusing the consciousness of the killer and the victim invites the reader to consider how we have all been programmed to be complicit in the murder's crimes.

Is the Well Running Dry?

S. T. Joshi

ROSS E. LOCKHART, ed. *Cthulhu Fhtagn! Weird Tales Inspired by H. P. Lovecraft*. Petaluma, CA: Word Horde, 2015. 315 pp. ISBN: 9781939905130. $19.95 tpb.

The spate of neo-Lovecraftian anthologies (and other works, now extending to novels and even plays) shows no signs of abating, and there may reason to wonder whether the market for this kind of material may be flooded. Despite the controversies surrounding some of Lovecraft's personal views, interest in his work has never seemed to be greater—but can we count on that interest (like the housing market) to continue on an ever-upward trajectory, or will there be a crash someday?

On the basis of the anthology *Cthulhu Fhtagn! Weird Tales Inspired by H. P. Lovecraft*, that crash may be coming—and perhaps should come.

If there is any overarching theme or agenda in *Cthulhu Fht-agn!,* it is that the entirety of Lovecraft's work—not just his so-called "tales of the Cthulhu Mythos"—is now fair game for the pastichist. In some senses this is a welcome development, since the number of elaborations upon "The Dunwich Horror" or "The Shadow over Innsmouth" (a story that has seen at least three volumes of imitations, as assembled by British editor Stephen Jones) would seem to be limited. Nowadays, virtually any story from Lovecraft's pen can serve as a springboard for imaginative rumination. The question remains, indeed, whether sufficient imagination is being brought to the task.

Ross E. Lockhart does not get the book off to a good start, writing a windy and contentless introduction in which he bizarrely asserts that houses are somehow central to Lovecraft's vision (missing the point that cosmicism—the depiction of the boundless gulfs of space and time—is Lovecraft's signature contribution to weird fiction). He compounds his difficulties by offering a lineup of largely unknown writers—and then failing to provide biographical notes on these figures, some of whom have actually done more creditable work than the few "name" writers he has managed to include.

One of the interesting phenomena we see in these stories is the degree to which Lovecraft himself—or, at least, the not entirely accurate image of Lovecraft as the gaunt, lantern-jawed figure stalking the streets of Providence, Rhode Island, at night—has become a fitting subject for fictional treatment. The book's first contribution, Walter Greatshell's "The Lighting Splitter," is a mad story of what happens to a family that takes up residence in an 1861 house in Providence where Lovecraft had reportedly been a frequent visitor. I am not certain the story has any true coherence or plausibility, but its transition from a routine haunted house narrative to something much more bizarre and cosmic is effectively handled.

Quite a bit less successful is Nathan Carson's "The Lurker in the Shadows," in which we are asked to believe that Lovecraft continued living into the 1970s and came into correspondence with the young Stephen King. This alternate-reality tale, in which Alfred Hitchcock directed a film version of *Cool Air* and in which Lovecraft met Lord Dunsany in Ireland, is all very amusing; but its flippancy—and its unconvincing attempts to imitate Lovecraft's epistolary prose—condemn it to the status of an in-joke.

Lovecraft's "dreamland" stories—stories written early in his career, largely inspired by Lord Dunsany—have not served as the basis of many imitations, perhaps because they are imitations themselves. But Gord Sellar, in "The Return of Sarnath," has written a striking elaboration of "The Doom That Came to Sarnath," in which a band of fighters led by Terea, a warrior princess, and her slave Ajal (an unfortunate name, as it is too close to Atal, a character who figures in several early Lovecraft tales) are confronted by the rebuilding of Sarnath by unknown hands, centuries after its destruction by the reptilian inhabitants of Ib. While somewhat long-winded and meandering, the tale becomes strangely compelling, as Ajal exercises his powers of dream to cast his mind back into the past, in the course of which he sees Cthulhu emerging from his underwater city of R'lyeh.

W. H. Pugmire, one of the leading voices of modern Lovecraftdom, delivers a reliably evocative tale in "Into Ye Smoke-Wreath'd World of Dream"—a tissue of Lovecraftian allusions, where "The Call of Cthulhu," "The Terrible Old Man," and "The Haunter of the Dark" are all summoned. And the tale's cosmic and prose-poetic ending can only be quoted:

> I rose, like some monster of myth, with a stained glass city of titan blocks and sky-flung monoliths behind me. I wept, because I would no longer taste the mad dreams of the acolyte in my embrace. I groaned, because I could not flex my heavy wings and rise out of the water that was not my cosmic element. And I raged, because I could not see the stars through which I had filtered in antediluvian aeons, those stars that I would terrify so that they crawled through the chaos to the baying of Nyarlathotep, those shuddering stars that would align so as to spell my appalling name.

In sad contrast, Michael Griffin's "Delirium Sings at the Maelstrom Window" is a pretentious and incoherent riff on "The Music of Erich Zann," while Orrin Grey's "The Insectivore" is a lackluster tale based on the idea broached in "The Shadow out of Time" that beetles will be the dominant species on the planet after the demise of humanity. Michael J. Martinez's "On a Kansas

Plain" trots out the hoary idea that the Cthulhu cult—and the entity it worships—are real after all.

The longest story in the book is also close to the worst. G. D. Falksen's "The Curious Death of Sir Arthur Turnbridge" is a corny and verbose melding of the old-time detective story (with its hackneyed use of a know-it-all Belgian detective, Hieronymus Nos, an obvious stand-in for Hercule Poirot) with various Lovecraftian motifs thrown in at random, ranging from "The Rats in the Walls" (Captain Norrys figures as a character) to "The Hound" (there is talk of ghouls, a jade amulet, and so on).

Not much better is "The Curse of the Old Ones," by Molly Tanzer and Jesse Bullington. This is an attempt at Lovecraftian humor—a very dangerous mode to venture upon, for it is fatally easy to end up sounding like an idiot. Here we are asked to believe that a British film called *The Call* [or *Curse*] *of the Old Ones* starring Peter Cushing, Vincent Price, and so on was once in production—but if the film is ever completed, then mankind is doomed! Let it pass that the authors do not know how to spell the central character of "The Dunwich Horror" (whom they habitually render as Wilbur Whatley, rather than Whateley). This is the least of the story's problems. A fictitious entry in a reference book about the film unwittingly provides a perfect synopsis for the story itself: "Incomprehensible mishmash of several stories by H. P. Lovecraft."

The difficulty with a number of other stories in the book is that they may or may not be competent weird tales, but their connection to Lovecraft is highly problematical. For example, Richard Lee Byers's "The Body Shop" is a grim and grisly post-apocalyptic story about aliens having taken over the earth—but the aliens don't seem to be specifically Lovecraftian in any meaningful sense. Anya Martin's "The Price of Lyghes" is a tale of "extreme horror" that comes uncomfortably close to sadism, as we are forced to witness what appears to be the author's unholy glee at the dispatching of a cheating and abusive husband at the hands of some nameless entities he has apparently secured (by mail!) from the South Pacific; but I derive no Lovecraftian ambiance from it at all.

T. E. Grau's "Return of the Prodigy," written in a tiresome hipster prose that relentlessly makes fun of its unsympathetic protagonists, depicts an elderly couple that takes a belated honeymoon to an island in the South Pacific called Walakea (veteran readers of Lovecraft will immediately identify this name as that of a character in "The Shadow over Innsmouth"). There is plenty of disgusting horror on display in this story, but once again I do not sense any vital relation to Lovecraft.

The worst offender in this regard is Laird Barron, whose "Don't Make Me Assume My Ultimate Form" concludes the book. This is one more reprise of what has become something of a shtick in Barron's output—the commingling of the superhero topos with that of espionage, with a certain amount of physical gruesomeness along the way. Here Barron seeks to provide some variation by having his superheroes be a group of strong women (or, as he calls them, a "cabal of kick-ass bitches"—a term I presume is meant in praise). One of these individuals heads up to Alaska, encounters a talking marionette in the shape of Edgar Allan Poe, and does battle with two tough broads who also have a talking marionette in tow, named Bob (also called "The Eater of Dolls"). There are some fisticuffs along the way that leave all parties rather the worse for wear. I am not joking: this really is the plot—if it can be called that—of the story. Aside from the fact that there is not the slightest Lovecraftian content in it, the tale embodies what might be called authorial preening: Barron is so keen on showing you that he is a clever and innovative fellow (he has, after all, used second-person narration—even though such a device does not in fact work very effectively here) that the fundamental absurdity of the story escapes him. Perhaps we can charitably assume that the tale is a parody of some kind.

The problem of true relevance to Lovecraft's work even dogs what is unquestionably the best story in the book, Cody Goodfellow's "Green Revolution." This incredibly compelling tale of an ecoterrorist in Honduras manages to invest a clutching horror into plant life—especially in its unforgettable image of a tree that has engrafted human beings onto itself:

> And everywhere in its branches, she saw people.
> They lived in the tree, and they *were* the tree. Some ran up and down the trunk like squirrels, or brachiated from branch to branch like spider monkeys. Others were tethered to vines that joined seamlessly with their spines, playing out like extension cords as they snatched flying prey from the air, only to snap taut and retreat back into the green.

Others were little more than tumors on the trunk and branches. Their green skins were scaly and infested with fibrous growths, their bodies bloated to translucence, converting sap and nutrients by some weird internal alchemy into nectar for endless lines of thirsty workers.

But again, one has to ask: *Is this Lovecraftian?* In such a fine story the question perhaps becomes an impertinence.

It would be unfair to focus on the distressingly many tales in *Cthulhu Fhtagn!* that are either aesthetic failures or insufficiently Lovecraftian or both. The volume is redeemed by such things as Ann K. Schwader's "Dead Canyons," a heady science fiction tale about artificial intelligence that features many links with *At the Mountains of Madness;* Christine Morgan's "Aerkheim's Horror," a striking narrative in which Vikings battle with Deep Ones in Vinland; Cameron Pierce's "Love Will Save You," an unsettling story of some kind of plague that turns people into glowing spheres; Scott R. Jones's "Assemblage Point," a hypnotic (if at times alternately coarse and pretentious) tale that melds Lovecraft and Carlos Castaneda; and Wendy N. Wagner's "The Long Dark," a powerful science fiction/horror hybrid in which the last remnants of humanity are trapped on a remote planet and are battling a cosmic "world eater."

But there are so many clunkers in this anthology that we must regard it as a very, very mixed bag. I am in no way prepared to admit that the Lovecraftian well is running dry, but I do believe that editors of all such volumes (including myself) need to exercise considerably greater aesthetic judgment in determining what we embalm between the covers of a book.

I am once again forced to note the dispiriting absence of anything approaching competent copyediting in this volume—a perennial problem with the small press. We are here faced with such stylistic and grammatical blunders as split infinitives, the misuse of "like" for "as" or "as if" ("He wasn't getting over it like she'd hoped"), the superfluous "of" after "all" (one writes "all the time," not "all of the time"), the hideous barbarism "alright" (which immediately places a dunce cap on one's head), and all manner of other derelictions. The fact that many readers, writers, editors, and publishers are not even aware that the above *are* errors is a sad commentary on the present state of English usage. And there are some specifically Lovecraftian errors, as when W. H. Pugmire (of all people) writes the standard cry "Iä! Iä!" but leaves off the diaresis (umlaut) over the "a."

The demise of the English language is far more horrifying than anything depicted in Lovecraft's stories, or in the stories of any of his imitators.

A Love/Hate Relationship

Tony Fonseca

NICOLE CUSHING. *The Mirrors*. Vancouver, WA: Cycatrix Press, 2015. 221 pp. ISBN: 9780692442784. $19.95 tpb.

You are writing a collection of stories. As you travel along the path of your imagination, you come to a fork in the road. One sign points to a well-paved street with little to trip you up. It promises shorter fictional forays, with little worry about characterization, a place where idea is king and nothing else matters much, a route that can be easily traversed by a skilled writer—someone who can make stories that are tantamount to ideas read so beautifully that the casual postmodern reader does not even notice he/she is being short-shrifted. You look ahead and see that a fellow writer, Thomas Ligotti, has traveled this route so often that he has left signposts along that road for others to follow, so as not to get lost. You look at the other road, and there you see not so much a road as a treacherous path. Its dangers lie in the unfamiliarity of the landscape. It is a path that requires careful planning, forethought, and a determination to see the journey through. You pause only briefly before talking the paved road.

It's not that you really believe that "less is more." You know that this is an impossibility, simply an aphorism created by corporate-minded people who want to maximize outcome (in their cases profit) while putting in as little effort as is possible while still accurately claiming that you have made an honest go of it. You can try to make yourself buy into the writerly fiction that less can be said with more words, but you know that the truth is that good writing is good writing—certainly a masterful writer can say more with fewer words than can a hack—but that masterful writer can say even more if he/she so desired, and those extra words (and you know this because you are a masterful writer) would be as filled with wonder and would be as engaging as the words that preceded them. In your heart, you know that giving your readers more isn't really about taking away their ability to "use their imaginations"; rather, it is giving them a better glimpse into your imagination and inviting them to suspend their disbelief just long enough to play there. In essence, you want to hold their hands along their readerly journey, just long enough to get them to where they glimpse the darkness (since you're a masterful writer of the weird), and then you want to release their hands and invite them into your funhouse. . . .

And now here I must digress meta-textually and point out what you have already realized—that I have been experimenting with second-person point of view in a review. You, the reader of this, will form your own opinion as to the success of this experiment, most likely based on whether you believe the P.O.V. was necessary to get the point across, or whether you sensed that it was gratuitous, that it was experimenting for experiment's sake, that perhaps I am giving in to the temptation to be more clever or writerly. And this brings me to my review of Nicole Cushing's *The Mirrors,* a collection of twenty-two stories that seem to have as their aim to channel Thomas Ligotti in technique and style. Here, I will go out on a limb and state that, unequivocally, I have never had much use for Ligotti's tales or his style. I know this statement is anathema to many of my colleagues (and many of you readers), but in all honesty, I find his tales ponderous and storyless. They spend more time winking at themselves than they do establishing motive, character, or even a clear sense of an idea. I am not saying that Ligotti is not a prose stylist; in fact, I am saying the opposite, that he is a stylist, in the way that Henry James was a stylist. But a fair number of masterful sentences tied together by an interesting concept do not a story make.

And that is my beef with Cushing's collection. I want desperately to love these stories. Cushing is a thinker's thinker. After having read just three or four tales, readers may find themselves wondering if Cushing's isn't perhaps the most prolific imagination ever encountered. The concepts behind her stories in *The Mirrors* are nothing short of brilliant (albeit very, very dark—she not only visits the pit of despair, but she revels in it, dances in it, and examines every one of its elements in loving detail), but the execution of the stories leaves me wanting more. In some cases, it is because of her perceived need for cleverness (apparently for the sake of being clever). For example, I found myself questioning why is was necessary to tell a story of a couple faced with cancer and the inability to pay for a funeral from the point of view of a bottle of morphine. It made little sense when I read "The Truth, as Told by a Bottle of Liquid Morphine," and it continues to make little sense as I write about it. By the same token, I have to question the necessity of using second person throughout "The Fourteenth," another story about the death of a spouse and the grief of widowhood. With both of these stories, which show moments of masterful writing, I find myself asking if maybe Cushing sacrificed effect and raw honesty to cleverness, and this is not a good trade-off for the reader. The world is filled with MFA writers who can experiment with form and technique, but what it lacks are writers who can plummet readers into the depths of grief and despair in such ways that they feel changed by the reading experience. Every bone in this reviewer's body tells me that Cushing can be that brilliant author who makes you feel as deeply about loss as did Gabriel García Márquez in *Love in the Time of Cholera* or Gary A. Braunbeck in *In Silent Graves*.

The other issue I have with these stories—which, I remind you, I did fall in love with at first glance—is that they feel like cheats. In attempts to out-Ligotti Ligotti, Cushing cheats the reader and herself in "The Orchard of Hanging Trees," a tale that has such a brilliantly inventive view of hell that readers will be slack-jawed in awe when they experience it for the first time (and probably the second or third), and flirts (weirdly) with philosophy and the questions of life's meaning so well that I thought I was reading the next Robert Aickman; but the illogical need to keep the tale brief (doesn't anyone realize that less is always less, or have we all gone crazy or gotten lazy?) causes it to lose its steam. The brilliance of the concept is marred by the fact that the main character's epiphany does not follow from the tale's action—as if pages were somehow left off that would have explained how someone turns a selfish, lustful act into something genuinely character-changing. Likewise, "White Flag," about homelessness and despair through the ages, and "The Company Town," about suicide-as-solution (also seen in "The Cat in the Cage"), are much more sparse than they need be. In the case of all three stories, I would have gladly sat through even novella-length treatments (the writing is that good and the central concepts that engaging) had they been offered. But I did feel cheated. It was as if I sat down to read a screenplay and found myself staring only at a treatment: obviously I was left with more questions than need be after reading. While I will admit that in some cases a counter-argument can be made that I am arguing personal preference here, in some cases the need to finish a tale quickly did stand in the way of logic. After all, what thinking person fails to see the illogic of leaving a month's worth of food for a cat in a carrier before committing suicide? There are so many ways a cat so contained for that long would certainly die, a fact that completely undercuts the final irony of "The Cat in the Cage."

The longer selections do make for better overall reads and are in many ways the standout pieces in the collection. Although it is a bit over-the-top, "Eulogy to Be Given by Whoever's Still Sober" is one of the better stories because it is long enough to give characterization a chance. As contrast to the book's shorter tales, "Subcontractors" and "Non Evidens" offer the reader something they can sink their teeth into. There is an attempt to explain away some of the peculiarities of the stories in the "Story Notes," but the fact that story notes are needed does not bode well for the reader: stories should stand, or fall, by themselves.

Overall, I would recommend Cushing's collection despite its weaknesses and self-imposed limitations. After all, a talented writer deserves to be read. My hope as a fellow reader is that as her career continues, Cushing translates her brilliantly imaginative concepts to fuller stories and spends considerable time on motivation and character development. This would allow readers like myself to get to know the characters as people, rather than solely as images or instances of despair.

Revisionist Indigenous Horror

Chris Dallis

ADAM CESARE. *Tribesmen*. Portland, OR: Deadite Press, 2014. 114 pp. ISBN: 9781621051510. $9.95 tpb.

"The cannibal cycle, at its best, wants to horrify, sicken, and repel."

–Film director Jim Van Bebber (in *Eaten Alive: Italian Cannibal and Zombie Movies*)

When people think about disreputable horror subgenres, usually rape and revenge films like Wes Craven's original *The Last House on the Left* (1972), the grim epic *I Spit on Your Grave* (1978), and the sadistic nightmare *Thriller: A Cruel Picture* (1973) come to mind. However, when hardcore grindhouse horror fans really want to watch something visceral that will make them squirm uncomfortably with galactic fits of nausea, they will probably go the full nine yards and opt for an Italian cannibal film from the 1970s or '80s. Italian cannibal films, at their inception, were also influenced by the violent anti-western *A Man Called Horse* (1970), which features a narrative where a white man is incorporated into an Indian tribe that holds him captive and then introduces him to their unorthodox, bloody, and painful rituals. Italian exploitation master Umberto Lenzi, for example, all but remade *A Man Called Horse* in the first graphic cannibal film *Man from Deep River* (a.k.a. *Sacrifice!*, 1972). Ruggero Deodato then followed suit by riffing on *A Man Called Horse* in the film *Last Cannibal World* (a.k.a. *Jungle Holocaust*, 1977).

Allegedly anti-imperialist texts in intention, these exploitation films are more accurately described as a demented offshoot of the so-called documentary Mondo film tradition. Mondo films featured real (and, often, unconvincingly staged) looks at some of the more alarming and violent aspects of foreign cultures. The sensationalist marketing campaigns behind these films, which featured hyperbolic promises of unparalleled feats of brutality and awe-inspiring gazes at exotic sexual taboos, sold tickets faster than Luke Skywalker's land speeder racing over a dune while being chased by a pack of irate Tusken Raiders. Some of the other better-known aboriginal nightmare flicks are *Emmanuelle and the Last Cannibals* (1977), *The Mountain of the Cannibal God* (1978), *Cannibal Holocaust* (1980), *Eaten Alive!* (1980), and *Cannibal Ferox* (1981). Interestingly, a few directors of cannibal films—such as Umberto Lenzi and Sergio Martino—also helmed some of the most celebrated (and violent) giallo thrillers, spaghetti westerns, and Eurocrime films. Such was the nature of the Italian film industry: as soon as one exploitation trend faded, the talent then leapt into the next rising genre cycle to ride its wave from popularity to extinction.

Which brings us to Adam Cesare's amazing revenge novella thriller *Tribesmen*. Cesare pays homage to the Italian cannibal cycle by crafting a narrative about a European film crew that ventures out into the wilds of the jungle to film a horror flick. Of course, everything that can go awry does, which keeps readers constantly engaged and flipping pages. One of the great aspects of this book is how it appeals to aficionados of obscure film, film production staff, and horror fans simultaneously. Even if you've never seen an Italian gut-muncher saga, you will still value the work for Cesare's great storytelling skills. If you happen to be learned in cinema studies or film production, you will get a kick out of Cesare's sharp allusions to film history and his attention to detail when it comes to the specifics of cinematography.

Like *Ed Wood* (1994), which takes a disreputable exploitation filmmaker's life and spins it into a Frank Capra story, Cesare takes a splatter film director's new cannibal film project and then twists it into an adventure revenge thriller with unexpected twists and turns throughout. Or, for another analogy, like the Kill Bill franchise, *Tribesmen* takes a marginalized genre form, but then renders it intoxicatingly postmodern, resulting in an end product that transcends the parameters of the genre's original (and limiting) forms.

Tribesmen also scores points for the way it lampoons the entire film industry. When the director of the cannibal opus, Tito Bronze, proclaims that his project is "The world's first Neo-Realist splatter movie," readers will be reminded of Burt Reynolds's porn director character, Jack Horner, in the movie *Boogie Nights* (1997), who had equally outlandish pretensions regarding his work's cinematic importance. It is knowing moments like these that link Cesare's work to works that satirize sleazy media industries, like the film *Network* (1976), or Quentin Tarantino's original screenplay version of *Natural Born Killers* (1994), or the Roger Corman drive-in flick *Death Race 2000* (1975). For readers with interest in marginalized horror film forms, Italian genre cinema, satire related to media companies and their dubious products, or those who are just looking for an intense, ablaze, revisionist take on a genre chestnut, *Tribesmen* is a must read.

Just Like the Movies

S. T. Joshi

ORRIN GREY. *Painted Monsters & Other Strange Beasts*. Petaluma, CA: Word Horde, 2015. 200 pp. ISBN: 9781939905154. $14.99 tpb.

Orrin Grey likes movies; he likes horror movies in particular. This is not to say that he doesn't care for literature—the stories in his slim but worthy collection *Painted Monsters & Other Strange Beasts* draw upon elements from Poe, Lovecraft, H. G. Wells, and other writers—but his dominant influence, frankly and unashamedly acknowledged, is the panorama of horror films from at least as early as *Nosferatu* (1922) to the slasher films of our own day, with much in between.

As a source of inspiration for horror tales, one could do far worse. Many of the greatest weird tales—even those written long before the advent of film—have a cinematic quality that is a chief source of their power and vividness. It is no surprise that, amidst all the plodding prose of Bram Stoker's *Dracula* (1897), individual scenes from the book remain in the memory—and it is no accident that it is exactly those scenes that have become iconic in the leading film adaptations of that novel. Lovecraft may achieve his most pungent effects from his use of dense, richly textured language; but certain images in his work—the pursuit of the hapless protagonists by the amorphous shoggoth at the end of *At the Mountains of Madness* is to my mind the chief example—are imperishably visual and cry out for transformation on the big screen. And yet, Grey does not rely solely on image—or on nods to well-known horror films—to create an effective tale. The opening story in the volume, "The Worm That Gnaws," about two grave robbers (the technical term is "resurrection men") gathering recently buried corpses for the use of anatomy schools, is grimly powerful both in its use of what the author calls "Edinburgh grave robber accent" and in the appalling revelation made by one of the robbers—appalling precisely because he speaks of it so offhandedly—that he resurrected his own wife after she died suddenly.

Film imagery comes to the fore in "Night's Foul Bird," a brooding, atmospheric story that seeks, as the author states, to evoke "vampire imagery from early silent horror films." (I should note that the author has added explanatory notes to each story—a practice that I do not necessarily condone, since it creates too many opportunities for an author to seem pompous and self-important. Grey does not entirely evade these pitfalls, but on the whole his notes provide valuable clues as to the story's inspiration and overall direction.) "The Murders on Morgue Street" might be thought an ingenious riff on Poe's "The Murders in the Rue Morgue," with a nod to H. G. Wells's *The Island of Dr. Moreau;* but it is more an homage to the film adaptations of the works in question. "The Red Church" is an evocative tribute to the Italian giallo films—films that might seem to be more aligned to the mystery or crime/suspense genre, but which include an abundance of horrific imagery and at times even venture into the supernatural. Here the suggestion is that an artist creates exceptionally vivid sculptures—perhaps out of once-living subjects?

Perhaps the best story in the book is "The Labyrinth of Sleep," a poignant, hypnotic tale of a man who pursues a friend and colleague who has been lost in a dream world called the Labyrinth. The story was written for a Lovecraftian anthology, and it concludes appropriately on a note of cosmic menace. Not far behind is "Strange Beast," a fascinating and complex story about a group of filmmakers who are kidnapped in 1972 and forced to make a monster movie on a remote island, in the course of which the man playing the monster is killed—and strangely transformed. Grey effectively uses what in literature would be called the "documentary style"—a tissue of blog entries, excerpts from interviews, and other documents. In film lingo he is perhaps evoking the "found footage" trope. Whatever the case, the story develops increasing layers of richness and texture as it proceeds.

"Persistence of Vision" is a chilling but moving tale of the return of the ghosts of the dead *en masse* into the world of the living. While generally effective, the idea seems rich enough for a full-scale novel, and I for one would welcome Grey's making the attempt to write it. The same might be said for the long unpublished novella that concludes the book, *Painted Monsters*. Here, the premise of the story—the executors of a dead actor in horror films, Constantin Orlok, invite certain individuals to Orlok's estate in Mexico City for the reading of his will—sets the stage for a wild, histrionic narrative involving revivified corpses, meditations on the nature of the horror film, a certain amount of gunplay and fisticuffs, and much else besides. I'm not entirely sure the story truly hangs together, but it is not only an entertainment but, as the author states, a "whirlwind ride across horror's cinematic history."

Not every story, sadly, is effective. The events of "The White Prince" take place the year after the publication of the novel *Dracula;* and, although it keenly extends sympathy to a dying vampire, the story is too brief to have much impact. "Walpurgisnacht," published in a tribute volume for Laird Barron but actually written much earlier, is a confused, rambling story about a private party held on Walpurgisnacht on Brocken, a mountain in Germany made famous by a reference in Goethe's *Faust*. "Remains" is an implausible story about a serial killer who is also a sorcerer. "Ripperology," in which a Jack the Ripper scholar is killed by the shade of the serial killer, is narrated in too bland and languid a manner to generate any true suspense or terror.

This is Orrin Grey's second story collection, following *Never Bet the Devil and Other Warnings* (2012). He has also written a few chapbooks and edited some anthologies; and, of course, he writes extensively on horror film. He is clearly at the beginning of his career; and—aside from more than a sprinkling of annoying and needless grammatical errors—he can boast a prose style that is smooth, easily absorbed, and occasionally able to rise to the level of prose-poetry. His reliance on film as a source of inspiration might be troubling, but he has demonstrated the ability to absorb his influences and transmute them through the alchemy of his own imagination into something original and distinctive. I envision a bright future for Orrin Grey.

Lovecraftianism as Contagion

Darrell Schweitzer

STEVE RASNIC TEM. *In the Lovecraft Museum.* Horsea, UK: PS Publishing, 2015. 80 pp. ISBN 9781848638846. £15 hc.

Steve Rasnic Tem's *In the Lovecraft Museum* is a book you could almost justify buying for the artwork. Jason Van Hollander's wraparound cover is a brilliant success, a mixture of drawing and image-manipulation, in which readers see (on the cover) a room in the Museum in question, complete with a Deep One in one case and what might be the semi-dissolved remains of Wilbur Whateley in another, plus a rather elegant, steampunk-style Mi-Go brain cylinder, the Black Stone (from "The Whisperer in Darkness") and Something in a specimen jar, not to mention a long gallery of Lovecraftian portraits and art, containing repurposed Arkham House covers and others, even the cover of my own *That Is Not Dead* (2015). There are other odd and disquieting details, which repay close examination. What is so remarkable is how photographically three-dimensional it all looks, as if Tem's Lovecraft Museum actually existed.

Maybe it does, in some alternate universe, and inspired the story itself, which is about Jamie, a.k.a. James, an (apparently) independently wealthy man who never had much time for his young son and never took him to his favorite park after the boy's mother died. Years later, after the boy himself disappeared on a trip to England, our protagonist visits the park, finding it run-down, with a sinister history. (Hints of a depraved cult.) Meanwhile he begins to correspond with the head of a British H. P. Lovecraft Society, who invites him over to visit the new Lovecraft Museum being built north of London. He does, and frightening, surreal, and difficult to describe things ensue.

At this point we have a slight digression on the "rules" for a horror story. One alleged rule is that you should avoid lots of overt references to other horror stories and horror writers, lest it merely remind the reader that this, too, is just a story. Of course T. E. D. Klein famously trampled all over that one in "The Events at Poroth Farm," and Tem does a pretty good job of stomping it too.

Our hero lives in the same universe as you and I, one in which H. P. Lovecraft is honored as a great writer, in which aficionados of HPL also gravitate toward M. R. James and Arthur Machen—and one in which it would be fascinating if some rich eccentric (or several of them, it seems) really did build a towering Lovecraft Museum somewhere in the English countryside. It is not that the character inhabits (as far as he knows) a world in which Cthulhu and the Deep Ones exist, but one in which H. P. Lovecraft exists. It's an important distinction, and the starting point for any understanding of this novella, which then slides into less familiar territory. At the very beginning, a political poll worker comes to our hero's door and seems to sprout tentacles. Or something. Is it a hallucination? Is the rest of the story a flashback from this point, so that the tendency to see wriggling things everywhere is the *result* of the character's experiences? Or was he mad all along?

Ambiguity is often the soul of the supernatural story, and with it comes the question of the unreliable narrator. The novella is told in third person, but with a close-in focus from James's point of view, so when he goes on his trip to England and starts noticing things most tourists don't—like ragged, bandaged, rather odd-smelling people everywhere, and billboards in the underground showing uneasy-looking children holding unidentifiable pets—the questions of the protagonist's sanity and reliability are inevitably raised. His host, the oddly unfriendly head of the Lovecraft Society, doesn't notice any of these things. Or is he lying?

Is James's odd state of mind the reason he notices such things, or a result of his doing so? If he were merely independently mad, and if this were just about a crazy person who encounters the strange, the story be a lot less satisfying. Aesthetics demand that one phenomenon be related to the other. This is surely a rule of supernatural fiction too, a lot less readily ignored than the non-recursiveness one. It is basic to story structure. All the elements of plot and character have to create a unified whole.

Before this is over, the bereaved father has been encouraged to find his own path through the Lovecraft Museum and has pursued someone he is certain is his missing son, either conspiring with or compelled by his host. The Museum seems more than a Museum. It seems another reality, with sights and smells you would not expect in a mere tourist attraction, and, indeed, crowded with more visitors than one might reasonably expect. The host and son disappear. There is a complaint to the police about his behavior. (In interludes throughout the story, James is trying to explain himself to a police interrogator.) The police are not helpful in the matter of the missing son. The protagonist is suddenly and quickly shipped back to the United States, and he notices that the plane is filled with ragged, bandaged people. It soon begins to smell like fish.

So what are we to make of this? Does grief lead to hallucination or to an opening of the eyes to a new, forbidden reality? Has some kind of underground cult now become widespread in Britain, and is it using the Lovecraft Museum as a means of spreading some kind of contagion? Is this what was in the deeper background of the forbidden park his son was so fond of? ("Thirteen children killed," he is informed. "One of those wacko religious groups. They claimed that there was a race of creatures living in the countryside long before human beings came to be.") All these hints, as in a Ramsey Campbell or Robert Aickman story, build up to an outline, but Tem is not nearly as explicit as HPL himself would have been as to what we are reading into the tale. What he does do, very successfully, is build up atmosphere and manipulate disquieting details to suggest all manner of hideous possibilities.

Ramsey Campbell, Probably

MY NASTY YEARS

How much may change in a single lifetime! As we see the British releases of films seized by police from video libraries thirty years ago. Some—most recently *Don't Go in the Woods*—are no longer regarded as suitable only for adults, but for anyone over fourteen—I reflect once again on my experience of censorship. Perhaps it deserves two instalments of this column. For now, let me reminisce about the eighties, when the country saw an orchestrated panic about horror such as we hadn't seen since the crusade against horror comics three decades earlier.

Let me confess: I feel a trace of guilt about some of my behaviour back then. Perhaps in one case I ought to have known better, though admittedly this was at the start of the home video revolution. Our electrician friend, Neil Smith, asked me to advise on stock he should buy for a Betamax library he'd started with a colleague, who funded it with his redundancy pay. I can't now remember if they showed me a printed catalogue from which to help them choose titles, but I do recall my excitement when I visited a trade fair outside Manchester with Neil. One of these occasions made it clear that some films offered on home video were uncensored, very much unlike the versions previously shown in British cinemas. One distributor, Vipco, famously advertised some titles as the Strong Uncut Version with an exclamation mark—Fulci's *Zombie Flesheaters* was visibly restored, though I couldn't identify what had been put back into Tobe Hooper's *Death Trap*. Perhaps my recommending these films showed some commercial sense, but you may feel I was indulging myself by persuading the Amith partners (a name that took a syllable from each of their surnames) to buy *Eraserhead*. After all, this was long before Lynch entered the common consciousness.

The Manchester event would prove more significant than I knew at the time. Some distributors at the fair used advertising gimmicks, and the stall selling *Nightmares in a Damaged Brain* displayed a plastic brain in a jar to attract buyers. It caught the eye of Peter Chippindale, a journalist apparently alerted by a tabloid report to the existence of horror videos, which he pilloried in a *Sunday Times* article, "How High Street Horror is invading the home." It was illustrated with three video covers: the severed head in the refrigerator from Lamberto Bava's *Macabre*, the drilling of a victim's head in *Driller Killer* (used by Vipco to advertise the film in trade magazines, unwisely as it turned out), and a naked woman tethered upside down from *SS Experiment Camp*. We were sternly advised that extreme violence had "replaced" pornography as the video trade's most profitable commodity, a questionable claim and no doubt one designed to associate the two as equally deplorable in the ideal reader's mind. Before long the media were competing with one another to condemn the new avoidance of censorship, the more hysterically the better. Films that would have been taken for granted in their countries of origin—America, Italy, Spain—were declared obscene by Scotland Yard, and our politicians made haste to show concern. David Alton, a Liberal member of parliament, went so far as to suggest that no films rated as unsuitable for children should be made available for viewing at home.

There ensued years of police raids on video libraries. Some owners elected to sign away the cassettes that were seized, while others weren't given the option. Some ended up in jail, though when the case was tried by jury rather than by magistrate the offending items tended to be exonerated. Some video libraries simply hid titles that were likely to fall foul of the police, and a collector's market soon sprang up. In my experience most libraries would sell the cassettes they kept behind the scenes, and some even invited interested parties to browse the hidden shelves. Whether any police posed as collectors (as one officer did in the sixties when I offered de Sade's last novel for sale) I can't say. Soon enough the shelves were bare, and there had been nothing like enough copies to go round, so that people copied tapes for one another.

The method tended to be amateur, to say the least—simply hooking two video players together and copying the film onto a blank cassette. The results were, shall we say, lacking in clarity even at that stage of the game. Once the copy was itself copied—well, I invite you to visualise the result. It seems extraordinary now, in these days of the digital image, that anybody could put up with the smudged faded versions of films that resulted (although admittedly there were something like precedents: some 16 mm showings of films at film societies were pretty woeful, in my experience, and even theatrical showings could be problematical—a 70mm revival of Anthony Mann's fine epic *The Fall of the Roman Empire* revealed that the film had faded to sepia, an inadvertently expressive effect but hardly a welcome one). How desperate some of us must have been for our fix of uncensored horror!

Soon there were fanzines devoted to celebrating the suppressed films and their like. Some advertised films for sale, though seldom original copies, and before long such adverts were as likely to attract the attention of the police as of collectors. The police reaction was often excessive, even if you believed it was legitimate in the first place—legal tapes tended to be seized along with listed titles, whether out of ignorance or official malice—and the press coverage grew hysterical. One campaigner who enjoyed the attention of the media was Peter Mawdsley, head of

Liverpool Trading Standards. Let me not seem to denigrate his job—he was responsible for alerting the public to the sale of dangerous baby walkers, for instance—but it's a pity that he went after films. His office issued press releases about "criminal rings" dealing in banned videos—in other words, collectors swapping them or selling them to one another. I'm not sure if he or his office was responsible for circulating the notion that sales of horror films funded terrorism, specifically the IRA. He certainly went in for one trick often used in those days to turn the media against the offending films—showing the press a tape composed of the most horrific moments in them, shorn of context. Oddly, film reviewers weren't invited, perhaps because they might have been too well informed. I still recall one Radio Merseyside reporter's telling me after such a conference that I wouldn't have wanted to be subjected to such material, and describing in appalled terms the cannibal scene from Joe D'Amato's *Anthropophagus*. She wasn't pleased when I suggested that the scene belonged to an old Mediterranean tradition, and could be related specifically to Goya's image of Saturn devouring his children.

I'd already done my best to counteract the censorious panic in my film spot on Radio Merseyside, and now I took on a couple of Peter Mawdsley's press releases. One simply listed suspect films that Trading Standards employees were advised to look out for. I found it odd that in some cases a director's entire output was implied to be fair game for seizure—Dario Argento was one such. I raised the issue with a Trading Standards spokesman, who said that if they'd known I was so knowledgeable about films they would have asked me to help make up the list. I fear I would have been anything but helpful.

Mr. Mawdsley's most memorable press release consisted of descriptions of the most extreme scenes from four films his officers had seized. These included Pasolini's *Salò,* the Chinese *Men Behind the Sun* (a fiction film about Japanese atrocities in Manchuria), one of the *Faces of Death* films, and a fourth title that I fear has slipped my mind—not quite as memorable a document as I claimed, then. On the air I pointed out that the list conflated a work by a distinguished Italian director who had also made the finest cinematic life of Christ, a sensational but passionate film about real historical events, and a laughably and obviously fake documentary about injury and death. With unusual knowingness, the press release came with a photocopy of Steve Thrower's *Shock Xpress* review of *Men Behind the Sun*. Steve and our editor Stefan Jaworzyn weren't slow to react when I told them.

My novel *The One Safe Place* touched on the excesses of the video library raids. One protagonist teaches film at university and takes his students through *I Spit on Your Grave* (borrowing an approach from Martin Barker). His house is raided just as Ken Cowley, the author and book dealer, told me an actual lecturer's was. Years later I was really rather pleased to learn that Camille Keaton, star of *I Spit on Your Grave*, had enthused about the novel, and I was happy to authorise use of the relevant section as an extra on a British DVD edition of the film.

Towards the end of the last century uncertificated videos began to enjoy the odd status cannabis still has in Britain—illegal but easily available, and to some extent tacitly ignored by the law so long as its presence wasn't made too obvious. In the case of videos, film fairs were held in major cities and widely advertised. I still recall my astonishment the first time I went to one, finding numerous banned titles on tapes imported from Europe, together with films that had never been released in Britain. Not all the copies were legitimate—one stallholder tried to persuade me that a monochrome dub was of a film that had never been in colour—but most were. This helped me confront an infiltrator from Manchester Trading Standards, who insisted that the films were pirated and then, once I pointed out that the tapes he was condemning weren't, that they broke copyright law. He wasn't persuaded by my argument that presumably the American copies of books of mine on sale in a nearby Waterstones were equally illegal stock—of course I wasn't really objecting to them, quite the opposite—but perhaps at least he had to pause to think.

At the start of the present century events took an unexpected turn. In January 2001 *Zombie Holocaust,* a film in which not just the walking dead but cannibals get up to graphic mischief, was officially released uncut on British home video. It seems that, just as they had in the early nineties when they passed the hardcore version of *Ai No Corrida,* the classifiers were testing the public response. Although the tape boasted on its cover that it was uncut, I don't think anyone objected. The BBFC then set about allowing nearly all the previously banned titles, though a few—*Last House on the Left* was notoriously one—still suffered cuts for a while before ultimately surviving intact. I sometimes ponder how Peter Mawdsley feels about seeing the titles he pursued being made available in video stores. Perhaps his reaction resembles that of Elliott Ness in the de Palma film, who says that now Prohibition has been abolished he'll have a drink, but I wonder.

Very few films are banned in Britain these days, and those that end up that way are easily obtained from the likes of Amazon (or, if they're hard-core porn, online). The same is true of cut films, though often enough material for the theatrical release is restored on British home video. All the same, the years of the video library brought an unexpected aftermath. Ex-rental tapes, especially but not exclusively the banned titles, are sought by collectors with a passion we may well recognise from elsewhere—a fine VHS copy of *The Werewolf and the Yeti,* for instance, will delight video collectors as much as a mint early issue of *Weird Tales,* let's say, will chuff a pulp collector. So perhaps all the censors' efforts—not least those of the self-appointed campaigners and those who hopped aboard their vehicle—had a positive effect after all: they turned many of the films they attacked into minor legends. Otherwise some might well have been forgotten. Such are the whims of history, and part of the fun of the world.

The Mummy Walks, Again. And Again. And Again.

Greg Gbur

RICCARDO STEPHENS. *The Mummy.* Valancourt 20th Century Classics. Richmond, VA: Valancourt Books, 2016. c. 1912 (London: Eveliegh Nash). 246 pp. ISBN: 9781943910298. $16.99 tpb.

An ancient Egyptian mummy. An ominous and deadly curse. A growing collection of fatalities. It is a familiar and intriguing plot for horror novels.

However, many do not know that one of the earliest of such novels is Riccardo Stephens's *The Mummy* (1912). In fact, it has gone unread for quite some time. Until now. My favorite publisher, Valancourt Books, on March 1 released the first new edition of *The Mummy* in nearly 100 years. Straddling the line between mystery and horror, Stephens's novel presents an intriguing tale of death and obsession reminiscent of the exploits of Arthur Conan Doyle's Sherlock Holmes. The novel's publication was well timed to capitalize on what would become new-found enthusiasm among the general public for all things ancient Egyptian. On December 6, 1912, late in the same year the novel was released, German archaeologists discovered the bust of the Egyptian queen Nefertiti, which has become one of the most famous and copied pieces of ancient Egyptian artwork in the western world. (A new edition of Stephens's novel was printed in 1923 to capitalize on an even more spectacular find, the excavation of King Tutankhamun's tomb by Howard Carter in 1922; considering that tomb was hyped by the media as being protected by a curse, *The Mummy* was well-positioned for a spike in popularity.)

The novel begins as Dr. Armiston, medical practitioner and aging bachelor, is interrupted at breakfast by an urgent request. He is called in to consult on the cause of death of a man named Scrymgeour, who it becomes evident has died in an accidental fall in his home. The only peculiarity in the case seems utterly unrelated: in his home, Scrymgeour seems to have been keeping the mummy case of an Egyptian priestess. The case is closed as an accidental death, however, and this seems the end of the story—until Armiston is called in to consult on another fatality (also ruled death by natural causes) and finds that the same mummy case is present in the second victim's home.

Complicating matters, Armiston is soon called in to act as a consultant for a peculiar group of high-society individuals known as the Plain Speakers. The group's motto is that all present at meetings are free to speak their minds on any subject, on any person, without fear of repercussions (and under strict rules of confidentiality). What he learns is that this group has been playing a macabre game with the priestess' mummy, one that seems to have invoked an ancient curse inscribed on the mummy case. As more corpses pile up in connection with the game, Armiston vows to get to the bottom of the mystery, which may come at the cost of his own life.

As I have noted, *The Mummy* is an interesting novel that walks the blurry tightrope between mystery and horror. The closest comparison I can give to its overall feel and tone is Doyle's classic *The Hound of the Baskervilles* (1902); in fact, I would not be surprised if Stephens was partially inspired by this work. I also found the pacing and the mixing of horror and mystery to be quite reminiscent of one of my favorite authors, Stephens's Edwardian contemporary Richard Marsh. Marsh regularly wrote both horror novels and mystery novels, leaving readers of any particular book wondering—in a good way, I might add—what sort of story they were going to get. Stephens's novel is a somewhat slow-paced and leisurely read; readers shouldn't expect to find dramatic events and spectacular twists and turns on every page. Much of the book focuses on the curious habits and culture of London's upper class, particularly the members of the Plain Speakers group, and I found the conversations and intrigues of Edwardian society to be just as interesting as the mystery scenario. The solution to the mystery is revealed, or at least strongly hinted at, sometime before the conclusion of the novel—an interesting choice for Stephens to make, as it allows the reader to follow along and understand the specific steps he takes in order to pull back the curtain and reveal the wizard, so to speak.

Like most Valancourt releases, this edition of *The Mummy* comes with an excellent new introduction, in this case by scholar Mark Valentine, who writes of what little information we currently know about Riccardo Stephens. In addition, this volume has lovely cover art by M. S. Corley. Overall, the new edition of *The Mummy* is a must-own. For those who like mystery novels with a horror twist, or simply reading clever books set in Edwardian times, I can recommend it wholeheartedly.

Lively and Engaging Take on the Legend

Richard Bleiler

JUNE PULLIAM and ANTHONY J. FONSECA. *Richard Matheson's Monsters: Gender in the Stories, Scripts, Novels, and Twilight Zone Episodes*. Lanham, MD: Rowman & Littlefield, 2016. 268 pp. ISBN: 9781442260672. $80.00 hc.

Despite having written some brilliant work, Richard Matheson could be surprisingly uneven as a writer, capable of catching a moment of paranoid zeitgeist in one story while being unable to think through a situation or provide a convincing conclusion to another. Perhaps because he was also often unfairly dismissed as a genre commercial writer, or (again unfairly) pigeonholed as a horror/fantasy screenwriter, he has occupied a peculiar status: much of his early genre work has been discussed, sometimes at wearisome length, but he has also relatively rarely been the recipient of a sustained critical analysis. Pulliam and Fonseca's *Richard Matheson's Monsters* is thus a welcome work.

As its title implies, it is an analysis of the depictions of gender in Matheson's oeuvre. It is a consistently perceptive, lively, and well-written assessment, feminist in its approach, and its insights are many and appear completely valid. This having been said, the book is not quite perfect, and this review should mention that there are a few of the inevitable small spelling errors that creep into any project: Fredric Brown's name is misspelled in the text and spelled differently (and still erroneously) in the index, which is not quite as thorough as it ought to be. Similarly, the name of another writer supposedly known to Matheson, one R. J. Cox, appears, but I have no idea who this is. Nobody with that name appears in the various indexes to the pulp magazines readily available (and it is most certainly not an inadvertent inversion of the initials of the notable scholar J. R. Cox). And a sentence is repeated, probably not for emphasis but because editing missed it. This sort of thing is infrequent, generally trivial, and does not affect the enjoyment of Pulliam's and Fonseca's analyses. However, there are some odd word choices: the first mention of "Steel" (not referenced in the index) uses the term *android,* but surely

Pulliam and Fonseca meant *robot* or *machine,* terms they use in their more sustained and insightful analysis of this work. Their statement about the *Twilight Zone* episode based on "Steel" is that "the episode nevertheless is mired in 1950s gender role expectations, as is so much of Matheson's fiction." This occurs almost in passing, but, really, it is an important insight, one of many.

For all that *Richard Matheson's Monsters* provides a very lengthy, accurate, and seemingly comprehensive index of Matheson's published short fiction, there are a few issues that I wish Pulliam and Fonseca had addressed. It seems at times that Pulliam and Fonseca have bought into an "official" Matheson biography that has apparently never been challenged. Thus, with regard to Matheson's beginnings, they provide the often-repeated story that as a boy Matheson sent poems and stories to the *Brooklyn Eagle* (the local newspaper), which paid young authors in gold stars that could be redeemed for prizes, and quote that "because of the prizes he was able to get with his stars, Matheson joked that he was a paid writer by 1935." This is a nice story, a statement of youthful genius and drive, but alas, it does not appear to be verifiable. The *Brooklyn Eagle* is fully online, and Matheson's name does not appear in it for this period. This raises the question of whether Matheson was published anonymously or at all in the *Brooklyn Eagle*.

Next, in the context of discussing the stories, Pulliam and Fonseca provide very intriguing and insightful discussions of the names of many of Matheson's characters and how they contribute to the overall story. At times, however, I wish they had gone further. In their discussion of the different versions of Matheson's wonderful "Nightmare at 20,000 Feet," for example, they state that the 1983 motion picture adaptation changes the protagonist's name to John Valentine, who is "similarly represented as effeminate due to his fear of flying." They have previously noted that the 1963 William Shatner version of the story uses the name "Bob Wilson," a change from the original magazine publication's "Arthur Wilson," and they have noted and argued that the story involves a crisis of masculinity. Despite this, they have neglected to bolster their argument by mentioning the punning implications of Shatner's character's being named *Bob:* the crisis of masculinity begins with a mental illness, yes, but he has additionally been neutered and reduced by being *bobbed*. Bob Wilson's wife Christine's comment that "Mama's here" thus emphasizes what Pulliam and Fonseca refer to as "Wilson's lost masculinity" on several levels.

Finally, even though Pulliam and Fonseca recognize that Matheson's gender role expectations are mired in the 1950s, the narrative imagination in his longer works is often derivative of many earlier models and these tend to go unmentioned, as do his missed opportunities. Thus, *The Shrinking Man* owes much to the paranoias and psychosexual insecurities of the 1950s, but surely it is also indebted to the numerous earlier works utilizing this theme. Even if Matheson had not encountered the idea of a shrinking man in classic novels, he would have run into it in numerous pulp magazines and motion pictures, and he never seems to have recognized that what has happened once can happen again and that Scott Carey could have been only the first of a terrifying number of shrinking men from all walks of life. Pulliam and Fonseca are perhaps unduly gentle to their subject and do not take him to task for these issues.

Richard Matheson's Monsters is an important work, and Pulliam and Fonseca are to be commended for an astute job well done. Anybody who is interested in Matheson's creations and creativity, or the shows and media he came to represent, will find the volume lively, hard to put down, and thought-provoking in a most positive way.

Forget the Butler: The Mafia Did It

June Pulliam

TODD C. ELLIOTT. *Axes of Evil: The True Story of the Ax-Man Murders*. Waterville, OR: Trine Day, 2016. 157 pp. ISBN: 9781937584726. $18.15 tpb.

Little fiction or scholarship has been written about the notorious Ax-Man Murders. These murders took place between New Orleans, Lake Charles, Louisiana, and Beaumont, Texas, before World War I. This oversight is a little surprising in our culture, given the contemporary fascination with serial killers that began with stories of Jack the Ripper, which were circulated across the United States through William Randolph Hearst's newspapers. The relative lack of attention given to the equally grisly Ax-Man Murders has been attributed to two factors: most of his victims were dirt poor, and South Louisiana and Texas were not part of Hearst's empire. So local accounts of the murders were not circulated in national markets. Todd Elliott's *Axes of Evil* attempts to rectify this void by both identifying the killer and connecting him to several murders across the south and in the Midwest.

Elliott's book uses newspaper stories and police reports to craft a detailed historical account of the victims, as well as their communities' reactions to the grisly murders in which entire families were hacked to death or sometimes bludgeoned to death in their sleep with an ax that the killer presumably found on the premises. (Axes were a common household tool at that time, when most people hewed their own firewood.) Elliott identifies the killer as the Reverend Lyn George Jacklin Kelly, a destitute and fanatical itinerant preacher who traveled by rail to cities in the South in order to minister to the poor. Other historians have thought that Kelly was behind the infamous Villesca, Iowa, murders committed in 1912, in which Joe and Sarah Moore and their four sleeping children had their heads beaten into a bloody pulp with an axe, which was left on the scene. Kelly, who was described as a "sexual deviant" by a historian who connected him to the Villesca murders, had been caught peeping into the windows of people in the small Iowa town, and he was in the area at the time of the murders, though he was never charged with this crime.

While Elliott ties Kelly to a larger number of murders throughout a wider geographical area, he also claims that Kelly was *not* behind the murders dubbed the Ax-Man killings committed in 1917–18. Rather, Elliott claims that these murders were Mafia killings in which the perpetrator imitated earlier crimes in order to conceal his or her identity. Ray Celestine toys with this last theory in his mystery novel *The Axeman* (2015), in which a young Louis Armstrong and several other characters come into contact with the never-apprehended killer, who is indeed in the employ of the Italian Mafia. Rick Geary's graphic novel *The Terrible Axe-Man of New Orleans* (2010), a nonfiction account of the

Ax-Man's crimes, similarly speculates that the killings might have been Mafia-related. *American Horror Story: Coven* (2014) also perpetuates the story of the Ax-Man as the killer who terrorizing the Gulf South around World War I, linking the character to the infamous letter sent to the New Orleans *Times Picayune* in 1919 in which a writer who signed himself the Axeman demanded that that city residents of New Orleans "jazz it" on the night of March 19th if they wanted him to spare them. The letter turned the killer into a Louisiana legend, and interest was renewed by folklorist Lyle Saxon in his 1945 book *Gumbo Ya Ya: A Collection of Louisiana Folk Tales*. Elliott, however, is the only writer to date who has produced an entire book about the murderer and as well as claimed that Kelly was not, in fact, behind the most recounted of the Ax-Man's killings.

What's Lost Is Lost

Michael J. Abolafia

> "This [opinion that the earth rests on water] is the most ancient explanation which has come down to us, and is attributed to Thales of Miletus."
> —Aristotle, *De Caelo* [On the Heavens], 294a28–30

JOHN LANGAN. *The Fisherman*. Petaluma, CA: Word Horde, 2016. 282 pp. ISBN 9781939905215. $16.99 tpb.

Spanish Papers and Other Miscellanies Hitherto Unpublished or Uncollected, a ream of ephemeral writings by Washington Irving, legendary American chronicler of the fantastic, contains a minor essay entitled "The Catskill Mountains" that briefly—but with characteristic imaginative vigor—describes Irving's lifelong fascination with that desolate and mapless swath of hills, rivers, and ancient villages along the corridors of the Hudson. In the travelogue-cum-folk-history, Irving sketches the contours of a place that had long cast a wizarding spell over his mind's eye:

The Catskill Mountains, as I have observed, maintain all the internal wildness of the labyrinth of mountains with which they are connected. Their detached position, overlooking a wide lowland region, with the majestic Hudson rolling through it, has given them a distinct character, and rendered them, at all times, a rallying point for romance and fable. . . . To me they have ever been the fairy region of the Hudson.

Irving's cartography of the Catskills region is inextricably tied to his sense of the numinous. "Wild and romantic," the Catskills are "mantled with primeval forests," and Irving recounts his experiences listening to the unnerving fables of a trader, deeply familiar with the Indian lore of that region of the country, during one of his several voyages down the serpentine Hudson. The merchant related to him "Indian legends and grotesque stories about every noted place on the river, such as Spuyten Devil Creek, the Tappan Sea, the Devil's Darts Kammer, and other hobgoblin places," including "an old squaw spirit" who "had charge of storm and sunshine," and the "great Maintou or master spirit" who enlisted his familiars to weave clouds "out of cobwebs, gossamers, and morning dew." "Sometimes," Irving continues, "she would brew up black thunder-storms, and send down drenching rains, to swell the streams and sweep everything away," and the trader goes on to catalogue a vast store of "marvellous legends . . . about mischievous spirits who infested the mountains" that have "haunted [me] ever since."

And it's not just the Native Americans who whispered of strange necromancies and weird portents in the woodlands: the Dutch, too, regarded it as "a kind of wonderland," and Irving takes pains to document unusual stories of hidden gold deposits found and lost, of fleeting treasures lying just beneath the land's impenetrable, uninterpretable surface.

Although John Langan's new novel *The Fisherman* alludes to Washington Irving's work only once, the book is deeply haunted by the liminal borderland-zone that Irving conjures up in stories like "Rip Van Winkle." Known for his meticulous, elegant, and lyrical prose, Langan is frequently championed for his elevation of the contemporary horror tale into a thing not of lurid exploitation but subtle, mounting Jamesian unease. Langan's latest literary work—and his most thoroughly accomplished—is a welcome addition to a vivid modern canon of cosmic unease that includes the likes of such anti-luminaries as Laird Barron, Paul Tremblay, Michael Cisco, Thomas Ligotti, and Richard Gavin.

From its inception, Langan's novel establishes itself as an emotionally moving, sustained meditation on the anxieties of love and loss—forces ineluctable and all-consuming—and the ways that we shore ourselves up against the extremities of human experience. *The Fisherman* opens on a note of welcoming, though melancholy, frankness as we are introduced to the unpretentious, honest Abraham—or Abe, for short, an obvious echo of Melville's immortal lines in *Moby-Dick*—who, it should be said, is a genuinely convincing Everyman: he is prone to drink, an admirer of Dolly Parton and Hank Williams, a casual reader of novels by Louis L'Amour, and a man whose unphilosophical wisdom is strikingly and multi-dimensionally evoked by Langan's folksy, approachable style.

After being forced to bear witness to the slow-burn of his wife Marie's decline at the hands of an aggressive form of body-ravaging and soul-thinning cancer, Abe retreats into the dark demesnes of alcohol and isolation, a combination that proves nearly fatal—until he discovers fishing, or, more properly, until fishing discovers *him*. Langan's psychological explication of Abe's "cold February of the soul," his descent and ascent up and down the "rungs on the ladder of loss," is exemplary—his pitch-perfect and meticulously observed depictions of the vagaries of bereavement seem true to life and carry an unbearable weight that Langan expertly conveys through his silences and absences. Abe hears Marie's lilting voice in the backyard and, upon investigation, finds nothing but sunlight and trees. He sees her on hills and near rivers, but she evaporates always into aether—she is simply not there, no matter how much he wishes she were. As Abe contemplates:

> Some things are so bad that just to have been near them taints you, leaves a spot of baldness in your soul like a pare patch in the forest where nothing will grow. Do you suppose a story can carry away such baldness? . . . Can a story haunt you? Possess you?

Just as Abe is possessed and haunted by the unfortunate unraveling of his own life story—he repeatedly laments the future that he and Marie would never share, the impossible history he would never be able to recollect at life's end—so too is *The Fisherman* haunted and possessed by the past. Abe's angling offers him some measure of solace and respite, serving as a kind of outdoorsy balm of nepenthe, a productive means of channeling his languor and regret, *de profundis,* for his dream life (and wife) that never was. One of Langan's defining strengths as a writer is his willingness to embrace the world of everyday reality: in addition to his Everyman-like qualities, Abe works at IBM, and Langan's passing depictions of office drudgery, along with other moments of fleeting but memorable lightheartedness, serve to temper an otherwise wholly morose novel.

Abe comes to befriend his decades-younger coworker, Dan Drescher, who was himself driven into the uncharted sorrows of loss when a freak car accident claimed the lives of his wife and young children. Langan's depictions of Dan's mental decline are well drawn, despite his status as an ancillary character. Dan spends his long, lonely nights idling his car at the exact spot where his family died, and where (as Langan notes in a cruelly crushing detail) the township had only recently installed a traffic light—it was a dangerous intersection. In an effort to lift his coworker's spirits, and perhaps his own, Abe invites Dan to come fishing with him. They do, and become fast—though faintly uneasy—friends, their respective losses always hovering shadowlike in the background.

Langan has a penchant for atmospheric, scenic descriptions of the Catskills landscapes, and they are largely successful—invigorating, even—by virtue of his surprising, arresting prose. Langan writes, in an early scene from Abe's perspective:

> I don't know if you've spent time in the Catskills. . . . Up close, when you're driving among them with the early morning light breaking over their round peaks, they seem incredibly present, more real than real . . . and somehow you wouldn't be surprised if the mountain closest to you were to cast off its trees in one titanic shrug and start to lumber away, a vast, unimaginable beast. When you turn off onto whatever secondary road you need to take . . . opening every now and then on a meadow, or an old house, you think, *Here, there are secret places.*

Langan rivals even Irving in his uncanny ability to convene

the magisterial beauty—equal parts terrible and awe-inspiring—of the irregular, secreted countryside. Like Irving, who waxes poetic about the "sublime melancholy of our autumn, magnificent in its decay, withering down the pomp and pride of a woodland country," Langan revels in the distant forests and mist-enshrouded mountains that are themselves "characters" in the novel's grander narrative arc. In attributing an agency and *élan vital* to the natural world, Langan generates a creeping sense of suspense, intimating, like his peer Thomas Ligotti, that what lies beneath, or beyond, or behind, is a substratum of horror itself: horror as (dis)organizing principle, horror as (anti)life force.

As Jeff VanderMeer notes in his perceptive introduction to the Penguin Classics edition of Ligotti's *Songs of a Dead Dreamer and Grimscribe,* "Ligotti comments on modernity through the idea of ritual, and how ritual pervades our lives in both ordinary and outré circumstances. Ritual is a kind of mask that holds in check what happens in our most secret lives." Langan's explorations chart similar cartographies. Consider the following remark by a wine-drunk Dan during one of his late-night conversations with Abe:

> When I look at things—when I look at people—I think, None of it's real. It's all just a mask, like those papier-mâché masks we made for one of our school plays. . . . All a mask, Abe, and the million-dollar question is, *What's underneath the mask?* If I could break through the mask, if I could make a fist and punch a hole in it . . . what would I find? Just flesh? Or would there be something more? . . . Maybe whoever, or whatever, is running the show isn't so nice. Maybe he's evil, or mad, or bored, or disinterested.

The importance of this trembling Veil of Maya, though, becomes increasingly notable as the story progresses. In a high-Gothic maneuver, a large portion of *The Fisherman* takes the form of an inset narrative that ranges across centuries and continents. "The blast-furnace heat of revelation" that will all but consume Abe, Dan, and dozens of others is introduced via a frame-tale. During one of their upstate excursions to the mysterious Dutchman's Creek, the pair stop at an unpeopled, fishing-themed diner and encounter its owner, Howard, a failed writer, who, though reluctant at first, spends hours telling them all he knows about the ominous Creek and its doomed history.

The story, as it goes, was related to him by one Reverend Mapple, who heard it from Lottie Schmidt, who lived near the Esopus during the earlier part of the century, and who was directly involved in the place's latest incarnation of evil. The narrative that we have, Howard's Story, is set down from memory by Abe in a feverish frenzy. Always, like Henry James's *Turn of the Screw,* Langan's narratives defy easy truth-value assessment. In deploying the Gothic's age-old obsession with stories within stories, Langan communicates the fragility of narrative and subtly asks us to question the validity of tales long dissolved in the mire of memory, split into husks by time, slivered into fractions of what they once were in the hands of emotionally and mentally scarred narrators. As Abe says, "You might imagine Dan and I [*sic*] sitting somewhere off to the side of the drama that's about to debut . . . Or maybe you should imagine us walking the margins, watching the story unfold across the page."

The middle section of the novel leaps back in time to the heady, opaque world of the early nineteenth century, bringing to life the lost history of the small towns that spangle the Hudson's banks. Langan, in one of many apt narrative moves, writes these long-passed scenes in the present tense, which lends them an air of immediacy, connecting them intimately to the present world of Abe and Dan and Howard. A famous miser who lived in the area of present-day Dutchman's Creek, a prosperous merchant by the name of Cornelius Dort, they learn, loses his wife in ways that echo the plights of Abe and Dan. Yet the novel's true horror begins with the portentous arrival of a man known only as the Guest, a kind of wandering resurrectionist personage who touches off a maelstrom of local gossip. As the novel relates,

> There are a lot more storms than there used to be, or so the old-timers say, lots more thunderstorms, and don't they linger over the Station? Haven't the Dort house's windows been seen shining with a weird, blue light late at night? . . . There are stories that Cornelius has been seen, during a fierce summer storm, the lightning falling almost as fast as the rain, walking through one of his orchards, accompanied by a figure in black—not his Guest, no, this figure is distinctly feminine, wearing a long dress and a long, black veil.

Dort seems ageless; he lives past one hundred years of age,

and his Guest is seldom, if ever, seen for sure after his initial arrival. The novel enacts another temporal leap, fast-forwarding to the years leading up to the First World War. Langan introduces us to the Schmidt family, headed by the Teutonically stoic Rainer and his wife, Clara, and consisting also of their several children, Lottie, Gretchen, and Christina. Rainer and his kin are new arrivals to New York: they settle in the Bronx before Rainer opts to move them northward to find work as a stonemason with a massive damming project along the Hudson basin.

Throughout the narrative, Rainer's dim past is adroitly unfurled: he is a disgraced philologist with erstwhile Frankensteinian inclinations and Promethean ambitions whose promising career at the University of Heidelberg was cut short by the mysterious disappearance of his friend and competitive colleague, Wilhelm, after their dangerous delvings into books that yield secrets too terrible to name. The novel's temporal journey across three centuries, with uncharted eons lying in the distant background, is centered on the supernatural, necromantic experiences of Rainer, Lottie, Clara, and his sturdy fellow-workmen as they attempt to combat a nameless arbiter and conduit of cosmic dread that brings to life dead women and opens portals into cosmically destabilizing other-worlds, which issue forth from old Cornelius's mysterious stranger.

Langan's novel is interspersed with Lovecraftian tropes—German grimoires and *Schwarzkunstler* spellcraft; antediluvian texts, older still, arising from the primordial tombs of Egypt; thunderstorms as strange philters, heralding the intrusion of unplumbed worlds into our own; morbid Dutchmen, dwelling alone in isolated, crumbling stone manses; a mad painter whose portraits lead him to ruin—and the novel, it should be said, pays a great debt to Lovecraft's own Catskills horrors, like "The Lurking Fear" and "Beyond the Wall of Sleep." As Lovecraft writes in the former story:

> Fear had lurked on Tempest Mountain for more than a century. This I learned at once from newspaper accounts of the catastrophe which first brought the region to the world's notice. The place is a remote, lonely elevation in that part of the Catskills where Dutch civilisation once feebly and transiently penetrated, leaving behind as it receded only a few ruined mansions and a

degenerate squatter population inhabiting pitiful hamlets on isolated slopes. . . . The fear, however, is an old tradition throughout the neighbouring villages . . .

It would be inaccurate to call *The Fisherman* strictly "Lovecraftian," as its cosmic horrors would probably not fall in line
with Lovecraft's mechanistic materialism. Langan's terrors are
equal parts supernatural and existential. And beyond that: whereas Lovecraft's Catskills-dwellers are portrayed as less-than-human,
backwoods wastrels, rude approximations of human beings, Langan's are more fully drawn. The Schmidt family, as well as Rainer's companions—Jacob, Italo (and his wife, Regina), Andreas,
and Angelo—are possessed of a heroism and dignity that Lovecraft would seldom attribute to his out-of-the-way immigrant
characters. The effect is one of realism, humanity, and sympathy,
and the portrayals of Clara, Regina, and, in particular, Lottie are
noteworthy: they are fully formed characters with their own important roles to play in the terrors that unfold. *The Fisherman* is,
fundamentally, a story of redemption, although its resolutions are
far from neat, tidy, or expected.

One of the novel's most excruciatingly tense scenes involves
the young Lottie's confrontation with a resurrected woman in a
claustrophobic closet. As Lottie's narrative goes,

> Now, faced with the black ocean, she confronts a vastness that
> makes the Atlantic seem little more than a pond. . . . She has
> some sense of more, and bigger, beasts waiting beneath the wa-
> ter's surface, forms as immense as nightmare. The ocean is eve-
> rywhere. Not only does it stretch to the horizon in all directions,
> it's under everything as well . . . it's fundamental, as you might
> say. If what's around us is a picture, then this is what it's drawn
> on. . . . Lottie said it was like, if you could cut a hole in the air,
> black water would come pouring out of it.

Water as the basis of all existence, as the ontological groundwork
of Being itself, has a three-thousand-year-old history that yokes together the philosophical traditions of the Pre-Socratics, like Thales
of Miletus, as well as biblical stories of the Great Flood and the
Leviathan. And this passage, too, evokes Lovecraft's prose-poem
dream vision "What the Moon Brings," with its nameless narrator
describing his "crushing sleeping flowers with heedless feet" as he

runs both towards and away from a river dappled with lotus blossoms that "lure" him with their pale, dead faces.

One of the novel's focal ur-intertexts is Johann Wolfgang von Goethe's "Der Fischer," or "The Fisherman," a traditional Germanic ballad that provides the skeletal story for Langan's novel. The poem is worth quoting in full:

> The water rushed, the water rose
> A fisherman by the sea
> Observed his line in deep repose,
> Cool to his heart was he.
> And as he sits and listens well,
> The billow breaks and parts,
> And from the waters' churning swell
> A dripping woman darts.
>
> She sang to him, she spoke to him:
> "Why lure my kind away
> With human wit and cunningly
> To the deadly blaze of day?
> If you could know how blithe and free
> The fishes thrive below,
> You would descend, with us to be,
> And prosperous to grow.
>
> "Do not the sun and moon take on
> Refreshment in the sea?
> Do not their faces billow-drawn
> Loom twice as splendidly?
> This sky-like depth, it calls you not,
> This dank transfigured blue?
> Your mirrored form enthralls you not
> To seek the endless dew?
>
> The water rushed, the water rose
> And wet his naked feet;
> His heart with yearning swells and grows,
> As when two lovers meet.
> She spoke to him, she sang to him,
> His fate became quite plain:

Half drawn by her he glided in
And was not seen again. (Trans. Edwin Zeydel)

Admirers of the strange byways of literature will find echoes such as these throughout *The Fisherman,* which lend it a literary panache that elevates it beyond mere horror yarn. Langan's sources run deep.

At novel's end, Abe and Dan seem to enter Howard's narrative itself, and the centuries-long quest to reel in a vast horror becomes not just the stuff of history and folklore, but a monstrously immediate real-world, a present-day reality infected by the baleful curses and transgressions of the deep past. Langan's characters are constantly telling stories—about themselves, about their inner lives—while simultaneously becoming trapped *within* the stories of others, like Howard's, who is himself living in the shadow of what he has discovered from Rev. Mapple and ultimately from Lottie.

Although some of the characters feel a little too convenient—Howard, for example, is, beyond being a thinly veiled allusion to Lovecraft, a standard-fare stock character, the archetypal "ominous, hardened old man with a dark origin story to tell"—the novel's personages are, on the whole, genuine, real. Langan takes care to evince a degree of self-awareness when treating characters like Howard: Abe frequently remarks that he feels as though he is a character in a movie, which, to a degree, deflects some of the reader's concerns about believability and the "realism" factor.

The novel's crowning scenes of cosmic terror are not only unique, but so powerful in their ubiquity that they emerge as fully formed, constitutive almost of an entirely new mythos, folklore vivified and brought shockingly to life. Langan freely mines comparative religions—from biblical stories to Egyptian lore to Reformation-era Germanic occultism—to positive effect. His psychological portraiture is masterful, and his high-literary flair for metaphorical flourishes, combined with the novel's digressive, unaffected narrative style, make for a compelling, page-turning read. *The Fisherman* is a well-wrought, minor masterpiece that stands alongside the longer works of T. E. D. Klein and Laird Barron as an exemplar of what the cosmic horror novel, in the right hands, is capable of achieving.

Horrors in Winnipeg

S. T. Joshi

KEITH CADIEUX and DUSTIN GEERAERT, ed. *The Shadow over Portage & Main: Weird Fictions.* Winnipeg: Enfield & Wizenty, 2016. 283 pp. ISBN 9781927855362. $19.95 (Canadian) tpb.

I consider myself a reasonably cosmopolitan person—even a "citizen of the world" in many senses. But I cannot deny that my residence in the United States for the past fifty-three years has rendered me somewhat Americanocentric—someone who pays far too little attention to matters outside the shores of this cumbersomely large country. In our own little field, I am heartened by the emergence over the past several decades of a number of Canadian writers who have established themselves as some of the leading lights of weird literature—Richard Gavin, Simon Strantzas, Nancy Kilpatrick, Donald Tyson, and the poet Wade German.

The Shadow over Portage & Main presents an admirable array of work by writers who have some connection to the city of Winnipeg, the capital of Manitoba. It was a revelation to me that there even is such a phenomenon as "Winnipeg Gothic," but evidently there is. Many factors, both historical and meteorological, have brought about such a phenomenon. As Jonathan Ball writes in his preface: "Winnipeg the ruin, Winnipeg of the haunted past, Winnipeg of murder and flames. Winnipeg of cold and death, Winnipeg of the hopeless, Winnipeg the doomed." Who knew?

Few of the authors in this book have any significant reputation in the realm of weird fiction, but on the basis of their tales several of them ought to. Most of these writers are either academics or are practitioners of mainstream fiction—and that is probably why the majority of the stories utilize the supernatural to shed light on personal conflict rather than being pure "phenomena" stories where horror is external to the characters. The result, in many cases, is a depth of human feeling that is often lacking in many orthodox weird tales.

The stories cover a wide range of motifs and approaches. Some of them are not explicitly set in Winnipeg, but that city's chilly and forbidding atmosphere seems to lurk constantly in the background. David Annandale's "Body without Organs" is a moving tale of a man who is being haunted—because he himself is so empty inside. John Stintzi's "Keep Your Pants On" is a mad story about a man who has had sex with a woman whose belly then expands with unnatural rapidity, consuming her entire form. There is here an exquisite balance between humor and grisly horror. Joanna Graham's "Tapestries" tells horrifyingly of a man who makes a tapestry out of the corpses of birds and rodents, intertwined with living vines and plants—a grotesque fusion of life and death.

Richard Crow's "Waiting Room" is the haunting, mesmerizing account of an alternate world (or perhaps the world of the future) in which a man and his wife are involved in a horrible accident, whereupon the man is offered the chance to live by having his injuries somehow transferred to his wife. In Jeremy Strong's "The Weight of Thought," five young people discover a trapdoor in the woods. Opening it and descending into the depths revealed by it, they come upon unthinkable horrors and are forced to make dreadful moral decisions to remain alive. I did not find the story entirely plausible, but it was a strangely compelling narrative. Daria Patrie's "A Winter's Tale" is a twisted fairy tale about a wife (who may herself be a fairy princess) whose husband enjoys torturing women. The unpleasantness of the tale is simultaneously muted and augmented by the author's delicately prose-poetic idiom.

Each of the editors has contributed a long story. In general, I am not keen on the practice of editors contributing to their own anthologies, especially since in this case the two stories take up more than a quarter of the book; but in at least one instance the inclusion is justified. Keith Cadieux's "Stuck" is the grim tale of a young boy forced to sit for a photograph with his recently deceased mother. (The tale is set in the past, so that the whole procedure takes hours, augmenting the boy's trauma.) Later the photograph itself seems possessed, returning to the boy's nightstand even though he repeatedly puts it away. In spite of a somewhat simple prose idiom, the tale gains tremendous cumulative power. Dustin Geeraert's "Past the Gates" is somewhat less successful, being the meandering tale of two young men, excessively fond of drink and drugs, who run into a female shaman who claims to be in touch with some nameless entity she calls "the Hidden One." There are a few engaging nods to Lovecraft, but otherwise the tale is a bit unfocused.

Other stories are sadly deficient. Brock Peters's "Like Faltering, Lisping Tongues" is a slight account of spirits emerging out of a wood. Géza A. G. Reilly's "Known of Old and Long Familiar" is a poorly written and long-winded story about a man who discovers a bound typescript of *The Cancer of Superstition*—a work that H. P. Lovecraft and C. M. Eddy, Jr., were ghostwriting for Harry Houdini at the end of the latter's life. Here the text appears to be complete (in fact, only three chapters are known to exist), and causes its finder to suffer all manner of unfortunate mishaps. In Eric Bradshaw's "Mortal Coils," an optician devises a pair of spectacles that show everyone's bodies draped with hideous tentacled creatures. If this is a "phenomena" story, then it is lacking in verisimilitude; if it is meant to be something more, then the symbolism of the tentacles is not clearly worked out. A similar problem besets Christina Koblun's "The Darkness." In the depths of a Winnipeg winter, the narrator senses the presence of some nebulous entity emerging out of the darkness. But what is the purpose of the entity's existence, literarily speaking? What underlying moral or aesthetic point is it meant to convey? I can find none.

Other stories are so poor that one begins to question the editors' judgment in accepting them. Elin Thordarson's "Foxdream" is the pointless story of a famous athlete in 1906 who is in a serious car accident and dreams of a talking fox while in a coma. Aside from this hint of strangeness, I can see nothing weird—and nothing of any great merit—in this narrative. Josh Gerard Moore's "Into the Madhouse" is a crudely written story about a man and woman who break into a carnival at night in order to enhance the displays in a "Haunted Castle" ride. The story is full of gratuitous gruesomeness that serves little aesthetic purpose.

Somewhat better, but not entirely successful, is Zacharie Montreuil's "All Roads," a tale of sea horror set in some unspecified period in the past. A sailor on a ship sailing to the New World senses the presence of a strange creature both on the open sea and on an island where the ship lands—but the identity and nature of the entity is never clarified. There is, inevitably, something of a William Hope Hodgson atmosphere to the tale, but it is on the whole unsatisfactory, marred by lack of focus and jarringly anachronistic language.

I am once again forced to note that the absence of adequate copyediting has rendered several stories considerably worse than they could have been. Several of the authors desperately need help in certain points of grammar, syntax, style, punctuation, and even spelling (e.g., "straightjacket" for "straitjacket"), but the publisher has apparently failed to provide the assistance that could have saved them from such blunders.

Overall, however, this volume is a creditable contribution to contemporary weird fiction, presenting several tales whose elegance of prose, dynamism of conception, and penetrating portrayals of psychological aberration and human conflict lift them far above the realm of mere shudder-coining. After reading these stories, I am not entirely sure I have any desire to visit Winnipeg, at least in winter; but I will be happy to read more weird tales about it in the comfort of my well-heated study.

Bierce and "The Damned Thing"

David Goudsward

DON SWAIM. *The Assassination of Ambrose Bierce: A Love Story.* New York: Hippocampus Press, 2016. 390 pp. ISBN 9781614981541. $20.00 tpb.

A character as complicated as Ambrose Bierce requires a writer with both exceptional skills and an in-depth familiarity with Bierce. In other words, you need author and Biercean scholar Don Swaim. *The Assassination of Ambrose Bierce: A Love Story* is Swaim's alchemical blending of history and speculative fiction to produce a new look at Bierce, a writer who should be far more widely read than he is of late.

Literary icon Ambrose Bierce worked as a journalist, a short story writer, a pioneer of psychological horror, and, especially, a satirist. He disappeared in Mexico in 1913 at the age of seventy-one, while observing the Mexican Revolution. Bierce's biography ends with the assumption he died in Chihuahua, Mexico, but Don Swaim's novel has this arrival in Mexico as merely the start of a new chapter in Bierce's storied career. In this version, Bierce not only survives in Mexico, he interacts with leading figures in the Mexican Civil War. The danger escalates as he draws nearer to his objective—Pancho Villa. Villa, violent and unschooled, begins to bond with the literary raconteur over war stories, with Bierce recalling his involvement in some of the bloodiest battles of the Civil War.

After several brushes with death in war-torn Mexico, Bierce heads north, accompanied by his *nuevo amigo* Pancho Villa. With the taste of death so prevalent, they travel to a place purported to enhance life—the mineral springs of Saratoga Springs, New York. Bierce decides that since he is assumed dead, he will remain so. Living in a fashionable hotel under assumed names, Bierce unexpectedly falls in love with a young widow who is half his age. His encounters with "the Damned Thing," his metaphor for Death itself, continue to haunt him as his past begins to become more prevalent in his thoughts.

Swaim's adeptness at bringing Bierce to life is such that, by the end of the story, you regret knowing that the tale was historical fiction. The acerbic septuagenarian has become so real that the reader nonetheless wishes Bierce had indeed found that proverbial happy ending that he himself did not believe was anything more than a literary device.

Who's the Psycho Now?

Chris Dallis

CHET WILLIAMSON and ROBERT BLOCH. *Psycho: Sanitarium*. New York: St. Martin's Press/Thomas Dunne, 2016. 278 pp. ISBN: 9781250061058. $19.50 hc.

"The Ego is not master in its own house."
— Sigmund Freud, from *A Difficulty in the Path of Psycho-Analysis* (1917)

"Sometimes I think that psychiatry hasn't advanced all that much in the past fifty years. . ."

–Asylum staff member Marie Radcliffe,
from *Psycho: Sanitarium* (2016)

Chet Williamson's newest work, *Psycho: Sanitarium,* is equal parts murder mystery, critique of archaic methods of the treatment of mental illness, and (obliquely) an inventive reworking of various themes found in the German Expressionist film *The Cabinet of Dr. Cagliari* (1920). Since, at its core, the work is a murder mystery, any reviewer has to tread lightly, since revealing too much information will ruin the labyrinth of unfolding plot points, red herrings, and reversals—which are a pleasurable experience for readers to undergo. However, the following can be stated without ruining too much: the tale takes place right after the events in Robert Bloch's original *Psycho* (1959), and the narrative is set entirely within the walls of a sanitarium with a dubious past. The most cruel and unusual staff in the facility keep turning up missing, and everything from the institution's ghosts of former patients to Norman Bates himself are suspected.

Still, in true murder mystery form, other characters are made to seem suspect. Bates's brother Robert, for example, gives Norman his guarantee that anyone, staff or patient, who torments him within the facility will be paid back with violence. Curious also is Robert Bates's creepy claims of respect for Norman because he had the guts to actually kill people. The woman he stabbed to death in the now-famous and fateful shower was, after all, Robert rationalizes, a thief. Then there is also the head of the institution, Dr. Goldberg, who seems to delight in wholesale sadism, since his preferred method of treatment is shock therapy. This same character has fashioned a new form of healthcare called Spiritual Repulsion Therapy, a method of therapy with uncertain benefits—if only because they originate from this heartlessness.

One of the most fascinating facets of Williamson's novel is that Norman Bates is one of the few sympathetic characters. Bates is genuinely disturbed by the id-like voice of his mother in his head, and he valiantly seeks to silence her. In contrast, fellow inmate Ronald Miller has no guilt about his passion for rape, and, like Norman's brother Robert, he admires the fact that Norman has had the gumption to actually kill. In a cruel universe where most of the institutional staff, patients, and even his own sibling are morally askew, poor Norman Bates would not seem to stand a chance. However, he does keep his moral compass grounded amid all these potentially damaging influences.

This, in fact, is the question at the center of *Psycho: Sanitarium*. But there are no easy answers in such a complex and amoral world. Therefore, readers will have to pick up a copy of this new thriller to make their own determinations of right versus wrong and in the process find out if, in the end, Norman Bates succumbs to evil once again.

An Interview with Chet Williamson

Chris Dallis

Chet Williamson has recently published *Psycho: Sanitarium* (New York: St. Martin's Press/Thomas Dunne, 2016). As my review in this issue points out, this sequel to *Psycho* is a murder mystery that critiques archaic methods of the treatment of mental illness. The tale takes place right after the events in Robert Bloch's original *Psycho* (1959), and the narrative is set entirely within the walls of a sanitarium. The following is an interview with Williamson about the novel.

Dallis: You dedicate your new book to Robert Bloch, Ray Bradbury, and Richard Matheson. How did these writers influence you in your formative years? Do you still feel the pull of their influence today, or have you, over time, moved beyond their influence?

Williamson: Those three gentlemen are still very much with me, Bloch for his plain, clear style and precise plotting (he liked to say he constructed a story the way you construct a joke, starting with the punchline and working backwards to the beginning); Matheson for his sharpness and immediacy and beautifully informed characterization; and Bradbury for his sheer imagination and the poetry of his language. Before the narrative proper, *Sanitarium* has two quotes, one from the original work *Psycho,* and another one from Thomas Kyd's drama *The Spanish Tragedie.* The Thomas Kyd quote is entirely apt, given the themes of madness and revenge in both Kyd's play and *Sanitarium.*

Dallis: Do you see *Sanitarium* as a modern Jacobean drama of sorts in the form of a novel? Even Dr. Reed, for example, seems to be enacting revenge on the facility's archaic forms of treatment.

Williamson: I hadn't thought about it in terms of being a Jacobean tragedy, but if the doublet fits . . . The novel actually does have the tropes, and in a way the pessimism, of that genre. That particular quote has always been in my mind because of T. S. Eliot's use of it in *The Waste Land,* and it seemed to fit nicely as an epigram.

Dallis: For the benefit of any budding horror writers out there, can you explain some of the differences and challenges of doing original works versus doing licensed work? For example, is licensed work more difficult, due to the fact that there is an existing mythos that you have to show reverence for? Or do both forms of writing projects have many of the same checks and balances and processes?

Williamson: I'd done some licensed work before this—two books for TSR, for which I created my own plots and characters, and two Crow novels, one a novelization of the second film, and the other an original novel, as well as a novel based on a videogame (*Hell: A Cyberpunk Thriller*). Though they were enjoyable to write and paid well, I made up my mind not to do any more. I really didn't think they helped to expand my readership to any great degree, and felt my time was better spent writing work that was fully my own. But I changed my mind when offered the *Psycho* gig. As far as showing reverence to the original, I had no problem. I grew up with *Psycho* and Norman Bates. My parents took me to the film when I was twelve, and I bought the paperback right away, becoming a Robert Bloch fan for life. I think that's the key in doing licensed work—make sure you have an affinity for it. I related to the two Crow novels I did, because so much of my original work dealt with love and loss and redemption. *Mordenheim* (for TSR) was a great fit because I was able to essentially recreate the world of the Universal horror films, which I've always loved. And *Hell: A Cyberpunk Thriller* came at a time when my son and I were both heavily into computer gaming. But I'd never do a licensed work that didn't appeal to me on a basic level. For example, I could probably never write a comic book superhero novel, because I have no interest in them to begin with. But every time I've written a licensed work, I've tried to make it my own, and I put as much energy and hard work into it as I do into my fully original work.

Dallis: For *Sanitarium,* how much research did you do? And what types of things did you research? I read in another interview that you researched the grim conditions of mental institutions during the time period of the story. What types of discoveries did you make researching this topic and any other topics for the book, and how did this data find its way into the final work?

Williamson: First of all, I reread Bloch's original novels in detail, taking copious notes, though the first book was the one I concentrated on most, since the events of the other two hadn't yet occurred when the action in my novel takes place. In terms of psychiatric treatment in the middle part of the last century, I found a great deal online, but for sheer atmosphere, I watched Frederick Wiseman's documentary *Titicut Follies,* shot in a Massachusetts state hospital for the criminally insane. The film is a painfully real document of how patients were treated, and there's a force-feeding scene that is almost unwatchable. A good friend of mine was a medical resident in a similar facility, though not as long ago, and he was one of my first readers and had a number of suggestions to heighten the verisimilitude.

Dallis: Here's a regional question about some of the local color here in the Lancaster, Pennsylvania, area. Is the Stockyard Steakhouse that is mentioned on page 28 of *Sanitarium* a reference to the Stockyard Inn here in Lancaster?

Williamson: Yes, the Stockyard Inn can take a bow here. I figured there would be "stockyard" restaurants near Fairvale, since Bloch located it somewhere in the Oklahoma/Kansas/Missouri/Arkansas area.

Dallis: Where did you come up with the Spiritual Repulsion Therapy treatment in *Sanitarium*? Was that just an entire fabrication cooked up for the book, or was it based on some actual techniques your research uncovered?

Williamson: Entirely fabricated. Perhaps I should try to market it!

Dallis: Is Dr. Goldberg's cookie fetish in the book just a character tag? Or is there some kind of deeper subtext to that character detail?

Williamson: Yes, a character tag that tells us a bit more about him, with a final payoff during Dr. Berkowitz's final visit to Goldberg's office. Besides, *everyone* loves Oreos!

Dallis: I found the plot device of Norman's having a twin interesting, because it links to several themes in the book and fantastic art and mystery thrillers: duplicity, doubles, human duality, and so on. Was this just something you came up with for pragmatic reasons relating to plot, or did you intend this twin to be more symbolic and suggestive of human nature in general?

Williamson: It's necessary to the plot, of course, but I've always been fascinated by the concept of duality as it relates to twins and doppelgängers, which I used in my earlier novel, *Reign*. And the idea of Norman's having not only a twin brother, but a twin who was feared brain damaged at birth, yet turned out to be the *normal* brother of the pair, struck me as an interesting avenue to explore thematically.

Dallis: The idea that twins are bound psychically is another great theme in fantastic works. The films *Dead Ringers* and *A Zed and Two Naughts* come to mind. Were you riffing on any specific other works when you opted to use this device?

Williamson: Not really. None that I can think of. It's just another interesting trope I wanted to play with.

Dallis: Ronald Miller and Norman's brother are interesting characters because they are foils to Norman. Were these characters designed to contrast with Norman to illustrate that Norman's nature is pure, whereas Ronald's and Robert's are unhealthy natures rooted in evil?

Williamson: I did want to make the point that Norman is essentially an innocent. Though he's intelligent, I see him more as a child-man who never grew up. Bloch's (and my) depiction of him as a big, overweight kind of guy (in contrast to Anthony Perkins's more sylph-like portrait) makes me think Lenny in *Of Mice and Men,* and though Norman has the same capacity for violence, he has that vulnerability about him as well, and Ronald Miller and Robert Newman provide a nice contrast for those qualities.

Dallis: Was the character Dr. Goldberg based on anyone real? Or a composite of several real people? He's a pretty developed character with a rich and interesting background, so I thought there might be something there that was sparked by an actual person or persons.

Williamson: No, Goldberg is pretty much cut from whole cloth, though his love of opera reflects my own. I own all the boxed LP sets that he mentions.

Dallis: There seems to be an interesting link to sex and violence in *Sanitarium.* Ronald Miller, for example, has channeled his desire for revenge into the act of rape. And Eleanor and Myron seem to have found a way to channel his rage into lovemaking. Was this a conscious decision on your part to make an implicit statement about various forms of unhealthy sexuality and their links to violence?

Williamson: Absolutely. A quality of Norman that Bloch explores, and that I touch on as well, is Norman's wanting to have a romantic/sexual relationship. In *Psycho,* whenever he feels a sexual attraction to a woman, Mother takes over, and instead of seduction or rape the act becomes penetration by knife. So I wanted that sexually violent undercurrent to be present. Norman, for all his perceived and actual innocence, is a potential rapist even without (and perhaps *especially* without) the presence of Mother. One only has to look at Bloch's *Psycho II* for evidence of that.

Dallis: OK. Let's assume that *Sanitarium* is the first Chet Williamson book I've ever read, and I really love it. What can you tell us about some of your other works to entice us to read them as well?

Williamson: I'd suggest going to my website at chetwilliamson.com and checking out the *You Wrote What?* section to see which titles might appeal to you most. I do have two new collections out: *The Night Listener and Others* from PS Publishing and *A Little Blue Book of Bibliomancy* from Borderlands Press. Or go over to Amazon and grab an ebook or audiobook. I've narrated most of my novels on audiobook (as well as *Psycho: Sanitarium*), along with other novels by Jack Ketchum, Kealan Patrick Burke, Clive Barker, and many more. Among my novels, *Dreamthorp* or *Soulstorm,* if you like hardcore horror; *Second Chance* and *Ash Wednesday* are my personal favorites; and if you like crime and suspense, there's *Defenders of the Faith, Hunters,* and *McKain's Dilemma.* Something for everyone! Come visit my website, follow me on Facebook, and I'm @chetwill on Twitter.

Ghosts as Linguistic Processes

Alexander Lugo

MICHAEL CISCO. *The Wretch of the Sun.* New York: Hippocampus Press, 2016. 272 pp. ISBN 9781614981664. $20.00 tpb.

Whereas H. P. Lovecraft's fiction pushes Wittgenstein's famous adage, "Whereof one cannot speak, thereof one must be silent," to strange and terrible dimensions, Michael Cisco's new novel, *The Wretch of the Sun,* urges its reader to use everything in his or her ontological, and therefore metaphysical, toolbox to circumscribe (however confusedly) the weird within language. As such, the novel is a dense, labyrinthine, and hallucinogenic take on weird fiction, and a refreshing one at that.

Perhaps it would be wrong to suggest, as above, such a binary opposition between Lovecraft and Cisco on the basis of the extent to which they provide descriptions of their horrors. In the novel's preface, the author notes that the haunted house, to which this work is a sort of postmodern take, "must conceal a secret imperfectly, and it must be the secret itself that, by its very nature and not primarily through any other agency, persistently resists concealment." Indeed, even Lovecraft's talk of unutterable terrors and unreadable grimoires nevertheless presupposes some linguistic appearance, however dodgy, so as to become perceptible at all. This may come across as a tautology, perhaps, though nevertheless one little remarked upon.

For Cisco, the best ghosts, the ones that we know and fear, are those that are utterly incapable of keeping themselves unreal. If they could, those ghosts would not appear within the real, but, as fantastic literature shows, this is always the case. In this sense, Cisco reads the haunted house, and by extension the greater realm of weird fiction, from a Derridean standpoint; pure transcendental hauntings cannot exist. If they did, the open secret that enables a haunting to be known and feared could never expose itself: "the really excellent haunted houses are the ones in which nothing out of the ordinary ever seems to occur." Weird fiction, then, sustains itself on depictions of failures, horrendous truths that cannot remain within their own preternatural territory. And this failure, according to Cisco, is integral to the functioning of such venerable figures as the haunted house. One of the chief triumphs of *The Wretch of the Sun* is its exposure of this contradictory process, and its consequent blurring of the seemingly stable binary between the hidden and the overt in fantastic literature.

Readers who like their hauntings to resolve like whodunits must be warned. The mysteries of Sanglade, the principal haunted house of the novel, and Cimelia Cisterna, its surrounding area, are riddles that explicitly "can never be unraveled." To this end, Cisco illuminates yet another seemingly obvious axiom of weird literature when he provokingly asks, "Why should natural law bend to what appears to be at least human justice?" As any close reading of, say, a novel in the spirit of *The Castle of Otranto* will make clear, the haunted house tends to endlessly defer the reader's conclusive understanding of the open secret(s) that it flaunts. Instead, its horrors are "explained by means of unexplained explanations, which only open out onto deeper mysteries." The *story* (to stress the linguistic emphasis on the seemingly unutterable that permeates this novel) of a haunting is always already unstable, always already intransigent to logic and rational explanation. Its ghosts and apparitions cannot be reduced to reasons and explanations, though these recourses to logic may be all we have to approach them sensibly. But even if we've found out everything there is to know, even if we've appeased hungry ghosts, the hauntings live on in the stories we tell about them, and their ghosts perennially manifest themselves within the imaginations of their listeners and readers. In this sense, every haunting is a ceaseless instance of textual *différance,* ever delaying its own understanding and repose. In *The Wretch of the Sun,* Cisco takes great pains to expose literary hauntings as figures for the inexhaustible instability of textuality itself.

To that end, the novel is in no sense an "easy" read, and its preface should be read carefully as an interpretative model—or, perhaps more fittingly, a guide—to the plot's capricious twists and turns. After all, one would be hard pressed to make sense of the narrative's clamorous opening, in which several cops, including two ghostly "plainclothesmen," pursue a disorderly individual "standing on a bench, shouting, flourishing a handful of paper above his head," unless he or she were to approach it as the novel's first hint of its haunting's own open secret(s). However, we must keep in mind that, as the preface suggests, there is *no* model, no story, in existence that can simply reduce a haunting's horrors to some unquestionably precise understanding. And just as the plot quickly provides its readers with good reason to make use of the preface's axomial content, it simultaneously throws them into the utterly, irreducibly unknown. For starters, the name of the first apparent major character slips from "A" to "B" to "C," and so on, in singly increasing increments every time the narrator mentions him directly. Does this ceaseless, revolving chain of letters refer to the language of the "story" that the ghost clings to in order to appear? What can be said, in any binding sense, about this character's identity? Is he even a character at all? Perhaps this alphabet cop, with his constantly changing identity, stands as a textual mediator or mouthpiece for the infinitely variable reader. In one sentence, the narrator will describe "alphabet" as a subject that clearly performs actions in the third person, but in another, as is the case for numerous characters across the novel's span, the narrator describes his actions in second person or even as if they were commands for the reader: "He looks down at the shimmering body. . . . Turn the body by the shoulder." Is this simply poetic justice? For a novel that often seamlessly oscillates between conventional narrative structure and lurid metafiction, one cannot be so certain.

This may help explain the lack of any clear plot teaser in this review, as is the case for the novel's own back-cover description. What, at first, may appear as a strange, though nevertheless realistic, twist on the police procedural, with its churning alphabet cop, quickly becomes even more outré once the disorderly figure upon the park bench, once pursued, vanishes into the rescuing hands of a *personified sun,* leaving another man, supposedly different, shot dead at the crime scene. Returning to the guiding principles of the novel's preface, one must notice how the rough, natural facts of this particular narrative situation, as with any significant narrative event in the novel, cannot account for the supernatural elements of the scene in any sense that lends itself to absolute summarization. All we know is that a seemingly unarmed man, perhaps drunk, is shot for no clearly discernible reason by no clearly discernible source. The straight, denotative facts mean nothing. Here, the supernatural comes into play as a slippage in the crystalline mathematic grammar of the normal. These disruptions only grow less and less pellucid as the novel progresses, which leaves the reader reeling inside a veritable chaos of linguistic trouble.

To call this work fragmentary or uncoordinated, however, would be a gross distortion of the novel's intense emphasis on storytelling and language and their ceaseless, layered dissemination. As is appropriate for a novel that focuses considerable attention on paranoid students, secret police, and self-conscious ghosts, many of the confusions of the plot stem from its morbid fascination with narratives, including its own. If what appears to "alphabet" (i.e., the man saved by the sun) is, in fact, a ghost, it seems appropriate enough that, in order to manifest itself into a proper, and therefore failed, haunting, its secretive nature must persists past the initial material manifestation into the symbolic, linguistic realm of storytelling. In other words, it needs an audience, and in "alphabet's" case, that audience is, *at first,* his sergeant: "Z. repeats his story, describing in detail the appearance of the solar woman." Interestingly, "alphabet's" name-sequence completes one systemic cycle (A–Z) after he retells the entirety of his story to the police sergeant and supervisor. If this figure stands for those elements of language and storytelling that, though fundamentally unstable, may codify the transmundane, then it seems telling that the whole range, or story, of his alphabetized identity completes not upon the actual experience of the *haunted* (and I stress the past-tense nature of this phenomenon), but upon its being made known. A haunting cannot present itself as an eclipsed product of a past understanding once it becomes the subject of a story, after which it can only continue to *haunt* as it slides into the same language that we use to codify the utterly mundane. Via storytelling, a haunting becomes more than a rupture in the normal; it becomes a virus within it, completely indiscernible from it. One may read the remainder of the novel as a performance of this relationship between linguistic utterance and the activation of a haunting proper.

Stories play out into more stories; they float around, rearrange, and confuse the reader like the ghosts they describe. In but the first twenty or so pages of the novel, plainclothes killers, a sun lady, a dead body, a mysterious car, rubber bullets, a secret investigation, the alphabet cop's partner's rehearsed assurances, and numerous other questionable instances jumble together and trouble all sense of certainty, including that of the difference(s) between characters, subplots, periods, and stages of life. Nothing resolves, no loose ends are *ever* tied up. And yet, like the alphabet cop who, against the stern warnings of several department superiors, retells his story of the sun woman and the secret police to everyone at his station at the urging of a "voiceless voice," the novel's amorphous haunting has a blind, functional need to reveal itself and, in doing so, produces the contradictory convulsions of its narrative. In *The Wretch of the Sun,* we come to read ghosts, as with innumerable other aspects of a poststructuralist ontology, as linguistic processes: "we are accustomed to think of language as the instrument of consciousness, whereas it may be that language and consciousness are one and the same. As some people say ghosts are dissociated from bodies, but the ghost is not energy, while it is 'energy'—the word . . . itself."

With its insistence on language and textual conventions, Cisco's novel offers its readers an education in the semantics (it itself is a radical transformation of the signifiers that capture and construct hauntings) and time-honed figures of the haunted house novel. Channeling Roberto Bolaño's notion of an "unknown university" that encompasses both raw experience and the poetic imagination, Cimelia Cisterna's "illegal" university, Cthethostoa, serves, as with so many other characters, narrative speakers, and places in the novel, as a doubled representation of these overarching motifs. Students like Trudy Bailey, the novel's heroine, pursue a degree that "does not officially exist, but will have more actual weight with other scholars than a similar degree from one of the sanctioned colleges." The narrator describes the campus swimming pool/school as "baleful" with its "insect composite-eye windows of glass blocks and a throat clogged with trash and dead leaves," while its student body enjoys "prying the asphalt up" in order to reveal how "some bushes, and small trees even, have emerged from the exposed earth." Its haunted libraries, phantasmal professors, and clairvoyant students suggest that the education characters like Trudy seek is in the very structuralist poetics of hauntings that the novel exposes its own readers to.

For all its attention to functional linguistics and narrative conventions, *The Wretch of the Sun* is not to be mistaken for literary criticism. One of the novel's most intriguing characters, the curiously named Professor Crapelin, is described "as though he were always doing an impression of himself." We may take this idiosyncrasy and apply it to the peculiar activity of the novel itself, which functions as a constant impression of its genre, superimposing clichés and expectations to the point of near-unrecognizability, where the tropes and conventions of weird fiction and the haunted house appear out of the redoubled and redoubling miasma of distorted poetics like ghosts themselves, like horrors simultaneously fresh and decayed. In this sense, Cisco is something of a structuralist à la Roland Barthes; he makes a simulacrum of the haunted house "text" so as to reveal how it functions and then utilizes the operations of this structuralist poetics as horrors themselves. In an age of increasingly stale genre literature, Cisco take a step back in order to take a step forward, and mutilates the conventions of the fantastic and horrible in order to produce something freshly terrifying. On one hand, fans of the weird will enter Cisco's world knowing precisely *what* to expect and fear, but, on the other hand, they will not know *how,* they will fail to recognize what has been otherwise recognizable for centuries. We are put in the position of the child (himself a trope of haunted-house fiction) who strays from his fellows only to fall victim to supernatural horrors: "The boy doesn't know this part of town and wanders with an increasing fear and terrible freedom."

The Wretch of the Sun throws its reader into a world, suspended between realist mimesis and surrealist hallucination, that cannot reconcile the tension between the particularity and generality of its hauntings. The novel's acute sense of a vertiginous uncanniness that does not necessarily disrupt the stability of reality, but, instead, embeds itself within it in a functional, structuralist sense will leave readers in a state not unlike that of Cimelia Cisterna's inhabitants: "Throughout the modelsuburb, people panic, run through the streets, they drop dead, their bodies sprout agonizing wounds for no reason, their skin is torn by nothing, their blood pours down, they scream and claw themselves. . . . That is, they go about their ordinary, everyday affairs as usual." With the novel's conflation of particular and general conditions, one is left with the strange, disconcerting impression that Cisco's text describes nothing at all, nothing but baseline reality itself, but from the perspective of a pair of eyes glued to old mirrors that just so happen to be our homes, our schools, our lives.

The Time Is Here for Iron Man to Spread Fear

June Pulliam

SHIN'YA TSUKAMOTO, dir. *Tetsuo: The Iron Man*. K2 Spirit-Kaijyu Theater, 1989. DVD: Image Entertainment (USA, 1998).

Cult classic *Tetsuo: The Iron Man* is like no movie I have ever seen before. The opening credits bill Tetsuo as part of Shin'ya Tsukamato's "regular-sized monster" series, indicating that this film does not fit into the prevailing *diakaiju* type of monster film—larger monsters like Godzilla—prevalent in 1989 when *Tetsuo* was made. Instead, *Tetsuo* is equal parts body horror film in the tradition of directors such as David Cronenberg and part fetish film, and related in a black-and-white Expressionist style that is reminiscent of classics such as *The Cabinet of Dr. Caligari* and *Nosferatu*.

It is the story of a man known only as the metal fetishist, who inserts pieces of scrap metal into his body, presumably to make it "hard" in the manner of the elite athletes whose images decorate his apartment along with other pieces of metal. After cutting a gash in his thigh and inserting a rusty bolt in the exposed flesh, the metal fetishist grits his teeth and attempts to run on his augmented limb, believing that he has made himself into a homemade Six Million Dollar Man. Instead, he is killed when he is hit by a car driven by a salary man and his beautiful girlfriend. Then things get really weird when the salary man is "haunted" by the metal fetishist: his own skin erupts in boils that spring nightmarish metal appendages that eventually encase his body. The most disturbing of these is a mechanical penis made of a lethal-looking screw drill attached to a piece of flexible tubing. As the metal takes over the salary man's body, he begins to look like a homemade Robocop, imprisoned by an impenetrable exoskeleton that obscures all the body parts that define him as human.

The salary man becomes a machine rather like the Terminator, whose only purpose is to make the entire world like him. Like King Midas, the salary man's touch is lethal; it turns the living into metal. However, this metal quickly corrodes, as the metal fetishist who had passed this condition on to him had inserted a rusty bolt into himself. In a particularly poignant moment, the salary man's touch has converted his pet cat into a mewling thing whose body is being taken over by metal parts. When the salary man next meets with his girlfriend, he copulates with her to death with his spinning bore drill penis and then reanimates her into a metal thing. The two then set off to re-create the world through their touch, transforming all life on earth into rusting metal parts.

Tetsuo's plot follows the logic of nightmare, something that is reinforced by Tsukamato's Expressionist vision. While the film is related in Japanese with subtitles, the dialogue is sparse. The plot is related through the actors' facial expressions and body movements, as well as Tsukamato's chiaroscuro photographic compositions. The actors too seem to have some dance training, as their movements are more like Impressionist modern dance than anything natural. *Tetsuo*'s soundtrack also contributes to its Expressionist feel—it consists of the rhythmic sounds of metal striking metal in machine shops and construction sites. Finally, *Tetsuo* is prescient in its vision of apocalypse and of an iteration of masculinity that is necessarily alienating. The metal fetishist and the salary man share their need to repress the expression of all emotion save anger, something expressed in a fear of the feminine. The salary man is a type of machine made of flesh, expected to do his assigned labor quietly and efficiently. His dark suit, functional glasses, and standard haircut emphasize how he is as interchangeable as any machine part. The metal fetishist too is an extreme of masculinity—even before we witness his proclivity to insert pieces of metal into his flesh, his square frame and chiseled jaw emphasize his lack of femininity. The salary man's nameless girlfriend also emphasizes his masculinity. In the salary man's nightmare images of her, she is the abject maternal, a devouring mother with a deadly mechanical penis rivaling his own, which she uses to rape him, thereby rendering him effeminate. In life, the salary man's girlfriend is so accommodating of his horrifically transformed body that she impales herself on his prosthetic penis, quite literally losing herself in the service of pleasing him.

Tetsuo is one of those cult films that Westerners are not likely to be familiar with. I admit that I had not heard of it until my horror film students brought it to my attention and insisted that we watch and discuss it. Readers of this review should make the effort to watch this film too. Unfortunately, this won't be easy, since it does not stream on any services such as Hulu, Netflix, or Amazon Video, and the few DVDs of it are expensive and only play in Region 2. Fortunately, the full film is available for viewing, for free, on the Internet Archive (archive.org), which makes available films that are rare and in the public domain.

What Makes a Lovecraftian Story?

S. T. Joshi

ELLEN DATLOW, ed. *Children of Lovecraft*. Milwaukie, OR: Dark Horse Books, 2016. 367 pp. ISBN 9781506700045. $19.99 tpb.

This is the third of Ellen Datlow's anthologies of Lovecraftian fiction, following *Lovecraft Unbound* (2009) and *Lovecraft's Monsters* (2014), the former consisting of all original stories, the latter mostly of reprints. This new volume is also all original—and it betrays many of the same deficiencies that beset its predecessors.

In her brief and perfunctory introduction, Datlow speaks derisively of Lovecraft's prose style ("his prose was often clumsy and overblown"), echoing the strictures of Daniel José Older, who regards Lovecraft as a "terrible wordsmith." Datlow is apparently unaware that any number of distinguished scholars and critics—including Joyce Carol Oates, whom she otherwise venerates—have regarded Lovecraft as a master of poetic prose. Regarding his prose as the "worst" aspect of his writing, Datlow urges would-be Lovecraftian writers to "create stories using the best of Lovecraft (the terror of the cosmic unknown, and his vision) to explore new themes, new horrors." Let it pass that there are many other themes in Lovecraft's stories than cosmicism. The question is whether her authors actually deliver on these recommendations.

To my mind, in large part they do not. There are four types of stories in this book: (a) poor stories that have little or nothing to do with Lovecraft; (b) poor stories that are derived from Lovecraft's ideas; (c) reasonably good stories that have little or nothing to do with Lovecraft; and (d) very good stories that are genuine adaptations or elaborations upon Lovecraftian motifs. I wish that that fourth category were larger, but it isn't; instead, a distressing number of stories fall into the first category.

I do not wish to linger on this subset of stories, but my duty as a critic compels me to do so. The worst—and in some senses the most surprising—culprit is Laird Barron's story "Oblivion Mode." I am saddened to see the decline and fall of this writer, who began so promisingly with two outstanding story collections (especially the second, *Occultation* [2010]) and a very creditable novel, *The Croning* (2012). But he has apparently bought into the encomiums of his numerous devotees and now thinks that anything he writes is pure gold. This story's plot is a trifle opaque, but it appears to deal with the efforts of one Karl (born Karla) Lochinvar and certain others (including a talking dog) to battle some person named Baron Need in a nebulous fantasy realm (or perhaps some moment in the past, as Romans are mentioned at one point). To say that there is nothing even remotely Lovecraftian in all this is hardly necessary; to say that this is a real stinker of a story is something of an understatement. I am half inclined to think that Barron engaged in a literary experiment to see how bad a story he could write that would still sell. If so, he found Datlow a willing victim for his ploy, relying as she does on what vestigial reputation his name still carries.

Maria Dahvana Headley's "Mr. Doornail" deals with a wife who feeds her husband's heart to the nebulous creature of the title. Written in an arch, pretentious style that quickly becomes wearying, the story entirely lacks a Lovecraftian foundation—unless the random mention of a tentacle is a tie-in. Brian Evenson's "Glasses" is a curiously conventional story about a woman who sees a strange entity through a new pair of glasses. It is written in a flat, affectless manner that generates no sense of the reality of the events—and of course there is nothing remotely Lovecraftian in the narrative (although this story too features a passing mention of a tentacle).

In the second category there are also some notable misfires. Siobhan Carroll's "Nesters" is a mechanical pastiche of "The Colour out of Space," with the events transferred to the Dust Bowl of the 1930s. There is little or no attempt to do anything but retell the Lovecraft story in a different setting—hardly an exemplification of the "new themes, new horrors" Datlow is urging. We also have Stephen Graham Jones's "Eternal Troutland," a long-winded, meandering, unfocused story, written in execrably slovenly prose, about the unexplained murder of a veterinarian and the ghost of a dog. I am quite serious: this actually is the plot of the story. Is there a Lovecraftian element in all this? Not quite; but it is possible the author is making some remote connection to

Frank Belknap Long's "The Hounds of Tindalos," if we are to take seriously some characters' discussion of time travel.

Orrin Grey's "Mortensen's Muse" is a story about a silent film actress who becomes a model for a photographer who wishes to use her in a series of "grotesques" he is creating. In one picture is a "hairy and squat" entity whose existence is beyond explanation, and which later kills the painter. No reader is likely to miss the fact that this is a cheap ripoff of Lovecraft's "Pickman's Model," written in mundane prose utterly lacking in atmosphere. David Nickle's "Jules and Richard" also uses "Pickman's Model" as its source, but once again there is no elaboration of the basic idea: the story ends up being an unimaginative retelling of the tale. Richard Kadrey's "The Secrets of Insects" is an uninspired story about Nyarlathotep taking the form of a serial killer in California.

The third category I have identified—reasonably good stories with no Lovecraftian content—has only two items. A. C. Wise's "When the Stitches Come Undone" tells of a man who returns to his home in a rural region called the "holler" (hollow), as he reflects on a traumatic incident in his youth when a cousin was apparently killed. This tale mingles terror and poignancy in deftly written prose, but I cannot identify any Lovecraftian element in it. (Lovecraft once planned on writing a story about a "witches' hollow," and the plot-germ of it survives in his commonplace book; but it does not seem as if Wise has derived her story from this plot-germ.) Livia Llewellyn's "Bright Crown of Joy," which concludes the volume, is a deliberately fragmented mood piece— an end-of-the-world narrative in which global warming (or perhaps something more sinister) has decimated the human population and rendered the earth all but uninhabitable. Are we to think that the narrator's repeated utterance, *"He is coming,"* alludes to Cthulhu arising from his underwater city of R'lyeh in the South Pacific? Possibly; but Cthulhu is never mentioned by name, and in general I sense no true Lovecraftian content here. Nevertheless, Llewellyn's fine use of dense, poetic prose is a pleasure to read.

Children of Lovecraft is saved by four stories that both are masterful in themselves and genuinely use Lovecraftian motifs as an imaginative springboard. Gemma Files's "Little Ease" (the title refers to an English torture chamber where a prisoner "could neither entirely stand up nor entirely sit down") is the potent tale of a female pest control specialist who is brought in to rid a decrepit boarding house of some unspecified insects. In the course of her work she runs into an elderly woman who is involved in research on a cipher written in John Dee's Enochian language. Dee was, according to Lovecraft (and Frank Belknap Long, who originated the idea), the English translator of the *Necronomicon,* but this point is not mentioned in the story. Nevertheless, the tale is strongly Lovecraftian in overall atmosphere, alluding subtly to "The Rats in the Walls" and perhaps even to "Under the Pyramids," the memorable Egyptian story Lovecraft ghostwrote for Harry Houdini.

John Langan's "The Supplement" is to my mind the finest tale in the book. Here an elderly woman (a retired librarian) obtains a mysterious book from a dubious character; touching the book's pages somehow allows the woman to relive (and revise) critical parts of her past life. Her teenage daughter, who died of a heroin overdose, comes back to life, and the woman seems to spend years with her, taking part in her life as she marries and has children of her own. The story almost entirely lacks any *terror,* but is an inexpressibly plangent account focusing on the bitterness of grief and the simple pleasures of domestic life. Above all, it renders the now stale Lovecraftian motif of the "forbidden book" vivid and mesmerizing.

Not far behind is Brian Hodge's novelette "On These Blackened Shores of Time," where a young man's car falls down a deep sinkhole in a small town in Pennsylvania; both the man and the car simply disappear. The man's parents refuse to give up hope and remain convinced that he is still alive. They conduct some research, finding that the sinkhole is located over the site of an abandoned coal mine where some riots occurred in 1927. As this narrative progresses, both the terror and the poignancy of the scenario grow to an almost unendurable pitch, concluding with a dénouement that is both cosmic and poignantly human.

Caitlín R. Kiernan's "Excerpts from *An Eschatology Quadrille*" is one more tale—she has written many—that simultaneously fuses Lovecraftian elements with her own distinctive vision. This magnificently evocative story is derived from a throwaway line in Lovecraft's "The Shadow over Innsmouth" referring cryptically to "Mother Hydra" and "Father Dagon." From this unpromising source Kiernan weaves a tale that spans more than a century (and extends decades into the future) and an entire continent, focusing on a strange jade carving that sows madness and death. Here, again, is an actual *elaboration* of Lovecraftian motifs—cosmicism, archaeological horror, and the notion that widely disparate events are connected in a web of inexplicable strangeness.

But on the whole, I am forced to conclude that Ellen Datlow does not have any real sense of what is truly "Lovecraftian" in contemporary writing. It is as if she is using Lovecraft's name to assemble an anthology that would otherwise have no particular reason for existence. This volume might just as well have been called *Children of Weird Fiction.* Part of the problem is that Datlow seems to have a very narrow cadre of contributors whom she favors. Setting aside Ramsey Campbell and Caitlín R. Kiernan as nearly unapproachable masters of Lovecraftian fiction, the best writers in this vein are (in my judgment) John Shirley, Cody Goodfellow, W. H. Pugmire, Jonathan Thomas, Ann K. Schwader, Nancy Kilpatrick, and Lois H. Gresh. But not one of these authors appears in any of Datlow's three anthologies of Lovecraftian writing. Should she ever contemplate a fourth such book, it might be well to expand her stable of writers to include those who have actually done vital work in this narrow but fruitful realm.

The Genius of Guillermo del Toro

Richard Bleiler

DANEL OLSON, ed. *Guillermo del Toro's* The Devil's Backbone *and* Pan's Labyrinth. *Studies in the Horror Film.* Preface by Ivana Baquero. Introduction by Guillermo del Toro. Afterword by Fernando Tielve. Lakewood, CO: Centipede Press, 2016. 416 pp. ISBN 9781613471012. $40.00 tpb.

The movies of the Mexican director, writer, and producer Guillermo del Toro are stylish, sumptuously crafted, and beautifully acted, and this volume is neither the first to recognize this nor likely to be the last on del Toro's cinematic accomplishments. Nevertheless, it is likely to be recognized as a bit of a puzzle.

Centipede Press is known for its expensive limited editions; yet for all that this book has terrific contents and is lavishly illustrated, one would never realize these from an external examination. The cover art not only fails to entice, it does not even begin to do justice to either the contents or the subjects.

The book effectively has two parts. The first consists of ten essays on del Toro's cinema and his accomplishments, three of which have received prior publication, seven of which are new and original to the volume. All discuss not only the two movies of the title but also such related subjects as the Spanish Civil War; del Toro's earlier accomplishments, such as *Chronos* and *Hellboy* are of course mentioned, but they are not dealt with at length. More attention is paid to *Pan's Labyrinth* than *The Devil's Backbone,* but then, it is the better-known movie, receiving not only widespread release but also enormous attention and a number of awards, including three Academy Awards. At the same time, the criticism in this section concentrates not so much on del Toro's cinematography as on the vision that is presented; cinematic close readings are generally out and sociopolitical assessments predominate. The functions of specific characters are examined by several of the essayists: Dr. Ferreiro, the quietly heroic physician in *Pan's Labyrinth,* is mentioned a number of times, and Romana Cortese's "The Quest for Meaning in *Pan's Labyrinth*" deserves attention for not only discussing Dr. Ferreiro at some length but for its insights and sympathetic assessment. Nevertheless, as would probably be expected, Captain Vidal—the sadistic figure memorably and terrifyingly portrayed by Sergi López—attracts more attention from the scholars. Indeed, editor Danel Olson focuses on him in "Pleasing Spectral Fathers: The Mirrored Quests of Villains and Heroine in *Pan's Labyrinth,*" an enjoyable and lively essay that discusses why certain cinematic "black hats" are remembered. Also lively and informative is Jonathan Ellis and Ana Maria Sanchez-Arce's "The Unquiet Dead: Memories of the Spanish Civil War in Guillermo del Toro's Cinema," which links Captain Vidal and his atrocities to events that an uninformed audience might miss. As a conclusion, it is fair to state that while some of the essays are stronger than others, all are worth reading; all are likely to inform the curious scholar.

The second part of the book consists of twenty-one interviews, a significant number of which appear to have been conducted in September 2015, though one is as early as 2006. It is safe to say that these are of varying quality precisely because they tend toward uniformity and the uncritical. Eduardo Noriega—Jacinto in *The Devil's Backbone*—thus speaks for all when he offers adulatory praise of del Toro, starting with a statement that "Guillermo is someone we don't only admire, but love," and continuing with such comments as "he cannot stop thinking, drawing, dreaming, working . . . and he is so funny at the same time . . . on the set, he's so demanding, precise, very careful, yet generous. He's always asking a lot of you—but then, he is the one to be working very hardest [*sic*]." This is very likely so, but it is the role of the interviewer to get beneath and beyond such uncritical assessments; too often this does not occur, and the surfeit of positive statements can make one wonder if perhaps, just perhaps, these actors are refraining from negative comments because they are hoping for additional roles from del Toro and do not wish to be seen as biting a hand that might feed them again.

Finally, and sadly, the volume is unindexed, and the contents too often are inaccessible. While it is nevertheless worth acquiring and, again, offers much, one closes it wishing that the editors at Centipede Press had invested a little more in making the book a better product and worthier of its subject.

A Modern Master

David Goudsward

CHET WILLIAMSON. *The Night Listener and Others*. Hornsea, UK PS Publishing, 2015. 334 pp. ISBN 9781848638860. £25 (hc), £40 (signed hc).

The Night Listener and Others is Chet Williamson's second, long-awaited collection of short works, twenty-one stories and a novella. It is a kaleidoscope of stories, ranging from ghost stories to Lovecraftian terrors with side trips into black humor and psychological horror. At the end of the book, Williamson adds notes on each story, noting such details as the publishing history and the inspiration. Reading those notes, it is striking how much of himself Williamson has placed in each story. This is not to say that any story is biographical—at least I hope not.

"Season Pass," for instance, takes place in an amusement park that has expanded into something unrecognizably big and no longer familiar to local visitors, much like the evolution of Hersheypark of Williamson's central Pennsylvania. "The Pebbles of Sai-No-Kawara" and "The Blanket Man" require not only a trip to Japan for inspiration, but a traveler like Williamson, who ventures off the tourist trails to locales rarely seen by *gaijin*. One of the best stories in the collection, "The Smoke in Mooney's Pub," again requires both a knack with subtle horror colored by the countless hours of performing in pubs to create that subtle familiarity that only comes from personal experience.

Toss in new twists on Dickens and Wodehouse, add the ghost of Vincent Price, a touch of genealogical weird tale, and you will finish this book knowing you have read the work of a modern master of the genre. And this is not hyperbole.

How good is Chet Williamson at writing horror? Let's put it this way: he is now riding the crest of praise for successfully accomplishing the nigh-on impossible task of creating a sequel to Robert Bloch's seminal novel, *Psycho*. When your name is bandied about in the same sentence as Bloch, you have to be at the top of your game. *The Night Listener and Others* is further proof those accolades are more than deserved.

Editor's Column: Aickman's Women and Archetypal Horror

Tony Fonseca

To appreciate Robert Aickman's short stories, it is necessary to understand the tales in their contemporary context, particularly in respect to the sexual revolution of the 1960s and 1970s. His contemporary fantasist Angela Carter stated in her essay "Notes from the Front Line" that the two-decade era that marked the most recent wave of feminism was in effect "Year One" for women. In retrospect, Carter's words ring even more true than they did when they were published, given that women were discovering feminine powers linked with sexuality, a stronger political voice, and reproductive freedom. Unfortunately, the backlash that accompanied the discovery of feminine power resulted in a patriarchal urge to squelch it, leading to what Karl Stern in 1965 called the flight from woman. For some men, the issue was not so much one of power as it was one of fear. In *Danse Macabre*, Stephen King expresses this succinctly when he writes that *Carrie* was about male fear of women and women's sexuality.

Aickman's weird tales are a marriage of the E. T. A. Hoffmann or Edgar Allan Poe school of the grotesque and the Jamesian psychological horror tale—mixed with a little Hawthornesque romanticism. As Peter Straub noted in his introduction to Aickman's *The Wine-Dark Sea,* Aickman cannot be categorized at all because he seldom uses the conventional imagery of horror, nor is his aim to invoke fear of the supernatural or monstrous. This also ties Aickman's style with that of Ramsey Campbell, an appropriate comparison.

Nearly all of Aickman's tales were published between 1968 and 1980, and a majority of them examine men who have shunned the feminine because either they fit into Stern's "flight into work" pattern or because they have lost the real women in their lives to divorce or death. Some of his protagonists are simply of the type we might call a "real mother's boy," as the narrator of "The Swords" professes himself to be. Confused by gender issues and sexuality, Aickman's male protagonists often find themselves attempting to rediscover the feminine through their interaction with female characters that are anima projections; these projected females often manifest themselves as goddesses, but they lead to destruction, sometimes utter annihilation for Aickman's male protagonists, who fail to assimilate the power of the feminine into their own psyches. These male characters are both attracted to and fear feminine sexuality and the inevitable chthonic—the natural cycle of life and death.

Succinctly stated, Aickman's female characters are more symbolic than real. In "The View," for example, Carfax, one of

Aickman's workaday, Jamesian male protagonists, is charmed by a woman who, when he first meets her, is his version of the feminine ideal: "She stood there like a pre-Homeric goddess, or Greta Garbo in *Anna Christie*, her oilskin glistening, her hair streaming, her eyes shining, her voice soft but unfailingly distinct: unforgettable." When Carfax returns from Fleet, the castle surrounded by an ever-changing view, he is Aickman's version of Rip Van Winkle, his reverse Dracula, a man who has speed-aged, while life literally passes him by. The feminine in "The View" is, as in one of Aickman's earliest tales, "Ringing the Changes," associated with change, the passage of time, and, as in many of Aickman's stories, death. Aickman's male protagonists are almost always middle-class, middle-aged, individuated characters, but his women are obvious larger-than-life symbols—the marriage of horror imagery with Jungian archetypes. In other words, the women in these strange stories exemplify James Hillman's definition of the archetypal, as expressed in *The Dream and the Underworld:* an image as metaphor.

In Aickman's short stories in *Sub Rosa, Cold Hand in Mine, Tales of Love and Death,* and *Painted Devils: Strange Stories,* published between 1968 and 1979, the number of horrific women increases with the passage of the decade. The physical manifestations or individuated image—to use Jungian terms—of these women can be divided into four recognizable horror types: the harpy, the vampiric female, the Terrible Mother figure, and death personified. One could say that Aickman's women are projections of the eternal, as well as the *internal,* feminine. They are recognizable mythological symbols, and because his male protagonists are products of (and are immersed in) the culture of the 1970s, these feminine projections are often reified as the goddess figure—but not necessarily in the form of virgin, mother, and crone. Aickman, like Hawthorne, relies upon polarization, or duality, to symbolize the psychic and moral forces in battle. The goddess-as-woman in his tales therefore takes on the form of the dual goddess associated with the cycle of life and death. She becomes the Shiva-like (or Janus-like) creatrix/destroyer, as in "Ravissante" (1968), "The Fetch" (1972), "Raising the Wind" (1977), and "The Stains" (1980). Even in "Marriage" (1977), perhaps the best example of an Aickman tale where the goddess exists as a triad, the bulk of this story emphasizes feminine duality, as represented by the roommates Helen Black and Ellen Brown. Aickman's male protagonists in these tales view the feminine in diametrically opposing images related to virginity and promiscuity.

In "Ravissante," the polarization of the feminine occurs in the second section of the story, which is in the form of a document found by the tale's narrator. In this journal entry, the surrealist chronicles what seems like a dream-sequence journey to Belgium to view paintings by a deceased painter of the grotesque. Upon reaching his destination, he encounters the painter's wife, Madame A., a dwarfish old woman who attempts to seduce him (the goddess as sexualized crone). She succeeds eventually, by having the artist serially fondle the clothing and then the undergarments of a mysteriously absent figure she calls her daughter, Crysotheme. The tale ends with the artist's symbolic castration at the hands of the phallic/terrible mother; his final glimpse of Madame A. as he retreats from the house is of her waving a pair of shears in the air and inviting him back, perhaps to cut him down to size so to speak, as she has done with the many artists whose paintings she routinely dismisses. It is no accident therefore that Madame A., and here the A could represent the Greek symbol *alpha*, or the primary cause, is projected by the surrealist as an instrument of destruction. She destroys the creative impulse of artists through both derision and what seems a supernatural power to control the artistic vision. Perhaps she is the dark version of the muse, represented by the absent daughter: from destruction is born creation, and vice versa, given the events of the tale.

"The Fetch" is the story of Brodick Leith, who as a young boy grew up with a deathly fear of his father, which was intensified by his dependence on his mother. His mother, however, is often ill, and while she is on her deathbed, she is visited by her doppelgänger, the witchlike carlin (doppelgängers also play a role in "Compulsory Games," discussed later). The auld carlin, commonly known as the fetch, is a crone figure of Scottish folklore who visits the living when they are to meet their death. Brodick's mother fixation never disappears, remaining even after her death: it causes him to dislike his stepmother when his father decides to remarry, and it causes his marriage to Shulie, his first wife, to fall apart. The fetch reappears at the end of the story to collect

Brodick, right after he has an argument with Clarissa, his second and present wife, who has left him as well. Because Brodick cannot release himself from the maternal, he remains, like the surrealist in "Ravissante" and Laming Gatestead in "Marriage," fixated on the mother imago. Accordingly, the final woman in his life is the fetch, who represents the abyss, the world of the dead, the destructive aspect of the Great Mother. Like the Manitou (a manifestation of the archetypal female) in Peter Straub's *Ghost Story* (1979), the fetch shows her victims their own faces at death; hence, she is Brodick's psychic projection, just as Alma Mobley is arguably a product of the collective unconscious of Straub's Chowder Society. Because of his inability to escape the mother, coupled with his vision of woman as being completely other, what he calls a "different zoological species," the beauty of Brodick's early relationship with his mother transmogrifies into his "marriage" with the grotesque, the auld carlin.

"Raising the Wind," from *Tales of Love and Death,* could also be grouped into this category, though the Terrible Mother figure here would be nature personified, or Mother Nature herself. In the tale, Fillbrick, the narrator, a man who has been emasculated by marriage, agrees to help move the *Dorothea,* a Thames barge, for a newly married friend. He encounters an old hag who, like many goddesses, is associated with the water, albeit in this case the polluted Thames, and she takes him to a ruined church, where she apparently blows a sweet-smelling wind into an empty bottle. When later opened by the narrator on a windless day, the bottle releases the sweet-smelling wind, which moves the barge. Tragedy strikes, however, when the winds cause the barge to sink. The tale offers no answers to the riddle it poses, but the implication is that the old woman represents the duality of the maternal figure, the anima, and nature itself.

"The Stains" begins with an immediate reference to the chthonic in the form of death by natural causes; the opening sentence refers to the death, following a prolonged terminal illness, of Stephen Hooper's wife, Elizabeth. To escape his own grief, Stephen journeys to the countryside to visit his brother, the Rev. Harewood Hooper, who is an expert on rock growths and lichens. During one of his walks to Burton's Clough, Stephen sees a young woman who is dressed in such a way as to be indistinguishable from the natural scene around her. It quickly becomes apparent that the girl, Nell, is a projection, because she mirrors his every move: she glances up (although he casts no shadow) just in time to see him looking downward. She returns his wave, and when he purposefully runs across the girl on his way back to the rectory, the reader is told: "One might have thought that the girl had been waiting for him. She was standing at much the same spot, and looking upwards abstractedly." Her first question to Stephen is a telltale one, for she asks him if he is lost. She is his mediatrix of the unknown, a numinous being who will help him to find meaning when faced with the meaninglessness of his wife's death. Stephen quickly recognizes Nell as version of the feminine ideal, realizing that although Elizabeth was a big part of his life, "perhaps the greater part of him," she was "not mysterious, not fascinating," like Nell, who is described by Stephen as being "sweet, calm, and changeless." Nell, comparable to the ideal woman in Aickman's "The View" or Alma Mobley in *Ghost Story,* is later characterized by Stephen as a maenad or an oread. In the scene where he makes love to her, she becomes the covertly seductive child-woman, an obvious stereotype. She is the death knell, the fetch.

Like Henry Fern in Aickman's "Never Visit Venice," Stephen follows his death wish and actually begins to court death. He seduces Nell, thereby incurring the wrath of her mysterious and monstrous father, who along with her sister (never seen but often discussed) represents the repulsive side of death. The deep, clear spring—another example of Aickman's associating his goddess figure with water (and perhaps mirrors)—is brought to Stephen's attention by Nell and is a clear indication that when he looks at her he is actually looking into his own psyche. When he gets on his knees in order to look into the spring, we are perhaps to see in this a symbolic motion of kneeling at the altar of the goddess/anima figure, as the surrealist does in "Ravissante" when fondling Chrysotheme's dress, or perhaps indicative of a narcissistic male tendency to project his own feminine psyche onto woman. Stephen notices that "on the edge of the rising ground behind the girl stood a small stone house," one that he is sure was not visible before. This so-called house is encircled by flying birds, possibly vultures, that he is also sure was not visible before. In short, after looking into the mirror (water), Stephen becomes aware of his own role in the chthonic cycle—he realizes his mortality. This stone cottage with a dirt floor and only one door is likely a fore-shadowing of Stephen's future tomb. His death wish, metaphorically represented in his making love to Nell, leads to his eventual physical state of decay: afterwards, the mold-like substance "on the skin between her right shoulder and her right breast . . . a curious, brownish, greyish, bluish, irregular mark" is slowly transferred from her body to his body, even to his surroundings. "The Stains" is much less ambiguous than most of Aickman's stories because at the end Stephen's body is found in an advanced degree of decomposition, and his car is rusted beyond recognition, implying that his death may have actually occurred upon or before his first meeting with Nell, well before the intervention of her father.

"Marriage," more than any other Aickman tale, uses the symbol of the tripartite goddess in its depiction of women. Aickman, however, updates the goddess triad based on the women's movement, for instead of the traditional virgin, mother, and crone figures, he has Laming Gatestead objectify women into *the professional*, the carnal, and the phallic-maternal. In "Marriage," Aickman exposes the male failure to reconcile the professional and the sexual aspects of womanhood. The story begins when Laming Gatestead meets the ironically named Helen Black, a slightly austere, highly independent career woman who is described as having a marked bone structure, pale eyes, a pale complexion that is emphasized by her habit of wearing her hair off her face, and pale ears. She works for the civil service and is described by Gatestead as having a dry, bony hand and an expressionless face; her frigidity is further accented by the fact that she always wears "simple" dresses. When the two meet in a theater gallery, she is tellingly clothed in a simple black dress, which unfortunately plays up the fact that she is taller than Gatestead. It becomes obvious that Helen Black is Gatestead's projection of the feminine when her roommate, Ellen Brown, is introduced into the tale. During the story's sex scenes between Laming Gateshead and Ellen Brown and afterwards, he begins to see Helen Black everywhere, even when she cannot possibly be there. She may be his projected feminine self (she, like him, is attracted to sexuality but is unable to act on it or appreciate it), perhaps even his conscience, or even a projected version of his mother, with whom he still lives. During his first dinner date with Helen Black, Gatestead finds himself instinctively attracted to Ellen Brown, who is described as having large, brown eyes, dark hair, a gentle nose, and an elfin smile. She is always seen wearing jumpers and fawn skirts, Ellen Brown is the child-woman, the seductress or nymphet.

Moreover, she is a manifestation of the second aspect of the goddess. Besides being more beautiful and feminine than Helen Black, she is an excellent cook, and she concocts a brilliant meal with "no smell of cooking and no sign of overall or a tea-cloth." In addition, she has the potential to become maternal, for she works as an advisor on baby clothes. She is the flesh-and-bones representative of Levin's Stepford wives. She meets Gatestead by chance the day after the dinner party, and she quickly and easily seduces him, in broad daylight, so that despite his sense of propriety he becomes her willing consort as they have sex in a public park (in a scene that establishes Ellen's tie with nature). And, as in all the sex scenes between Laming Gatestead and Ellen Brown, Helen Black, the virgin figure manifested as the professional woman, takes on a mysterious, voyeuristic role (again the question is always raised as to whether she is really there watching, as Ellen Brown never sees her).

As the story progresses through Laming Gatestead's sexual encounters, he begins to die symbolically as he grows lame in one leg. Unfortunately, he lacks the ability to be forever reborn, as the son and/or consort counterpart can be, perhaps because he fears the feminine. Eventually, Helen Black decides to discontinue her voyeurism, and she tries to become a "suddenly sexual" woman. In a scene filled with pathos, she is rejected by a lamed Laming Gatestead. While attempting to follow him after he rejects her, she becomes his Eve and takes a literal fall down a flight of stairs. He, still on the run, immediately meets Ellen Brown, who greets him "like a mother," but when he goes to her for comfort, he discovers that she has a past filled with sexual promiscuity. Lamed physically, emotionally, and sexually, he returns home to *his* mother, who, because of her white dress, looks "like a bride." The story ends with the mother's climbing into bed with him, to comfort him in his despair with a symbolically incestuous embrace. Helen Black, Ellen Brown, and his mother become party to his self-destruction. Nothing in the story indicates that his climbing into bed with the woman who originally gave him life has the potential for rebirth; rather the action seems tantamount to his resigning himself to the grave (womb/tomb).

Through these character studies of the male psyche confronted with the possibilities of the feminine, Robert Aickman exposes the myth of woman-as-enemy. The symbolically castrated surrealist painter, the potentially twice-divorced Brodick Leith, Fillbrick the emasculated sailor, the widower Stephen Hooper, and the workaholic "mama's boy" Laming Gatestead fail to reconcile themselves with the feminine. They, to a man, suffer tragic or pathetic fates at the hands of the various personified manifestations of the dual or triple goddess. Each fails as the son/consort figure because each is unable to deal with the powers of the goddess-as-woman. For Aickman's men, displeasing the goddess is at best destructive, and often deadly.

A version of this essay first appeared as "Alone with the (Archetypal) Horrors: Monstrous Women in Robert Aickman's Strange Stories." *Aickman Studies* 1.1 (2014).

Five Decades of Labyrinthine, Blood-Spattered Gialli!

Chris Dallis

TROY HOWARTH. *So Deadly, So Perverse: 50 Years of Italian Giallo Films*. Baltimore: Midnight Marquee Press, 2015. 2 vols. (233 and 228 pp.). ISBN: 9781936168507 and 9781936168583. $49.95 each, tpb.

"Though [Mario] Bava was a giallo pioneer, Dario Argento remains the genre's maestro."

—Howard Hughes, *Cinema Italiano: The Complete Guide from Classic to Cult*

For cinephiles and fans of Italian genre cinema, it is now officially time to rejoice! Troy Howarth's recently published two-volume fifty-year overview of Italian giallo films, *So Deadly, So Perverse,* has now filled a titanic informational gap in the written history of European thrillers. Up to now, many fans of these bloody shockers had to fall back on the 'zine scholarship of *European Trash Cinema's Special Giallo Collector's Issue* to find material about these films. Alternatively, horror fans also had Midnight Media's two 'zine-like volumes, *Giallo Scrapbook* and *Giallo Scrapbook 2,* to find useful facts on these genre films. And, of course, various genre websites and 'zines would periodically run features on giallo films and directors that helped inform cineastes about this European film form.

While all the above-noted sources are fine, they are hardly comprehensive. Howarth has done everyone a huge favor by producing a vast study of gialli, starting with Mario Bava's 1963 film *The Girl Who Knew Too Much* (1963) and tracing the Italian film cycle all the way up to the 2013 film *Tulpa—Demon of Desire.* My only mild criticism here is that Howarth does not include an afterword that comments on the arthouse neo-giallo works of Helen Cattet and Bruno Forzani, but this is a very minor quibble, given the wealth of information contained in this two-volume set. In an introductory chapter in Volume 1, Howarth does mention the neo-giallo films of Cattet and Forzani, *Amer* (2009) and *The Strange Colour of Your Body's Tears* (2013), but never offers a critique of the films in the second volume. I would love to know what he makes of these arthouse homages to classic giallo horror texts, since, as this two-volume set of film reviews makes plain, he has probably seen over a thousand Italian genre films. However, in a recent chat with Howarth on Facebook, he revealed to me that he will soon be producing a third volume to the series in which he will give detailed reviews of other works inspired by these grim Italian shockers.

In the first section of Volume 1, Italian screenplay writer Ernesto Gastaldi tries to offer a definition of giallo. He is not very successful, and he seems to want to keep the definition nebulous so that the multifaceted form can include works as varied as the stylish and operatic works of director Dario Argento and the more naturalistic and gritty fare of helmers like Umberto Lenzi. Howarth, however, contributes a preface in which he tries to extrapolate upon Gastaldi's attempt at a definition. Next, the European film scholar Roberto Curti offers a chapter on the evolution of gialli from a pulp fictional form to a cinematic one. Howarth then offers a chapter on several cinematic prototypes of giallo films. Finally, Howarth crafts a chapter on films that seem to be gialli, since they have many of the characteristics of the form, but then explains why they lack certain key elements he finds essential to calling them giallo.

While all these chapters are illuminating, I offer the following definition of a giallo film, based on the various observations found in these introductory chapters. To me, gialli are graphic and narratively complex crime thrillers produced in Italy from 1963 to 2013. The term giallo refers to the Italian word for yellow, which was the lurid color of the pulp fiction book covers that inspired the filmic form. Italian giallo films are generally celebrated by hardcore horror fans who enjoy the chills and thrills and bloodiness they offer. These cinematic works were inspired by the portfolios of thriller pioneers Alfred Hitchcock, Fritz Lang, and Henri-Georges Clouzot. The English writer Edgar Wallace is also an oblique influence, due to the vast popularity of his crime thrillers throughout Europe. For horror fans, gialli are to the 1970s what slasher films are to the 1980s: opportunities to experience great peril and graphic violence without having to risk actual life and limb. For an American reference point, the thrillers of Brian De Palma—especially *Dressed to Kill* (1980) and *Body Double* (1984)—play out like American takes on the Italian giallo. John Carpenter's *Halloween* (1978) is another reference point, though it lacks the key mystery element common to most gialli, that of not knowing the identity of the film's killer until the final act. While I'm sure fans and scholars of gialli might find some fault in my definition, it at least offers those interested in exploring the form some idea what conventions inform the films.

But back to Howarth. In Volume 1, he begins a year-by-year review of the films. While *The Girl Who Knew Too Much* is considered the start of the giallo cycle, Howarth correctly observes that it is not until Bava that the giallo started to mature and come into its own. Howarth notes in his review of Bava's timeless genre classic *Blood and Black Lace* (1964) that this was the first giallo that truly revolutionized Italian horror cinema and pointed the way for later auteurs such as Argento. Both Bava and Argento are amazing visual stylists, and their penchant for combining artful visuals with scenes of extreme violence would signal an entirely new aesthetic in European thriller cinema. Howarth's review of the surrealist and David Lynch–like giallo *Death Laid an Egg* (1968) is spot-on when he observes that "every now and again, avant-garde filmmakers would try their hand at something commercial like a giallo." The film's director, Giulio Questi, also turned the spaghetti western genre on its head when he helmed the bizarre and bloody European Western *Django Kill . . . If You Live, Shoot!* (1967), so it is no surprise that he made one of the most odd and amazing giallo films in the cycle.

Howarth also notes that certain giallo film narratives were imaginatively cross-fertilized with the then popular poliziotteschi genre, gritty Italian crime films influenced by the popularity of American neo-noirs like *Dirty Harry* (1971) and *The French Connection* (1971). One giallo/poliziotteschi hybrid that Howarth gives props to is director Fernando Di Leo's film *Naked Violence* (1969). This film's hardboiled look at juvenile delinquency and the life of the poor makes it an unusual giallo film, since it has a social conscience and is not just a series of chills and thrills. Howarth is entirely up-to-speed on his Italian genre cinema, so he features a sharp writeup on Lucio Fulci's masterful reworking of the novel *Vertigo* (1958), *One on Top of the Other* (1969). There are also fantastic writeups on Fulci's other exceptional giallo works, such as *A Lizard in Woman's Skin* (1971), and his socially conscious masterwork *Don't Torture a Duckling* (1972). In regard to Sergio Martino's contributions to the form, the reviews of *All the Colors of the Dark* (1972), *The Strange Vice of Mrs. Wardh* (1971), and *Torso* (1973) illustrate why he, along with the better-known Bava and Argento, is also a director whose works scholars and fans of the giallo will want to check out.

Volume 1 also has a review of Argento's world-historic giallo *The Bird with the Crystal Plumage* (1970), correctly noting that it would become one of "the most important films in the development of the giallo." The giallo/poliziotteschi hybrid *Death Occurred Last Night* (1970) is given a great review, noting that, like the gialli *Naked Violence* and *Don't Torture a Duckling,* it is informed by a social conscience. Bava's brilliant work *Five Dolls for*

August Moon (1970) is given a good review, despite the fact that Bava always dismissed it as a work-for-hire hack job. Howarth correctly notes that the film's theme mirrors the ones found in Bava's other celebrated films, *Blood and Black Lace* (1964) and *Twitch of the Death Nerve* (1971). In the review of film *The Black Belly of the Tarantula* (1971), Howarth notes that the film is "one of the strongest gialli of its period," despite also noting that it's a cash-in on the types of films Argento was producing at the time. Howarth notes that Lenzi, who is generally celebrated for his poliziotteschi and macaroni combat (i.e., "men on a mission military films"), also produced two noteworthy gialli: *The Oasis of Fear* (1971) and *Seven Blood-Stained Orchids* (1972). And Italian poliziotteschi-master Massimo Dallamano is justly given a shout-out for his chilling giallo *What Have You Done to Solange?* (1972).

Volume 2 immediately proves its value to giallo fans by noting a work that most have probably never heard of, *Puzzle* (1974), which was directed by Duccio Tessari, who did two other noteworthy gialli but is perhaps best known to Italian genre fans for his brilliant revisionist westerns *A Pistol for Ringo* (1965) and *The Return of Ringo* (1965). The review of Argento's tour de force *Deep Red* (1975) is spot-on, calling the work "murder as performance art." Luigi Cozzi's famed giallo *The Killer Must Kill Again* (1975) is given a complimentary writeup (Cozzi has also written the afterword to Volume 2, insightfully pointing out that that Sergio Leone's famed western *Once Upon a Time in the West* [1968] was a key influence on the giallo film for its non-linear jigsaw puzzle narrative). One of the sleazier gialli, *Strip Nude for Your Killer* (1975), is given a fair writeup, where it is basically noted that the work can be enjoyed as "kitschy entertainment" if not necessarily fine art. This film is of note to Italian genre fans because the director, Andrea Bianchi, also helmed the zombie film *Burial Ground: Nights of Terror* (1981) and the Eurocrime thriller *Cry of a Prostitute* (1974), cult films that no self-respecting Italian cinema fan will want to miss. Fulci's controversial giallo *The New York Ripper* (1982) is defended against the naysayers who panned it, yet Howarth does note that the work is "one mean bastard of a movie." The review of Argento's gem *Tenebrae* (1982) is justly gushing, though the writer finds the director's work *Phenomena* (1985) to be too idiosyncratic. While *Phenome-*

na is certainly not as good as Argento's masterworks *Deep Red, Opera* (1987), and *Tenebrae,* it certainly has a pronounced cult charm and is getting a new Blu-ray release from genre specialists Shout Factory, so Howarth's compass seems uncharacteristically awry here. The writeup on Argeno's *Opera* is complimentary, as one would expect it to be. Michele Soavi, who is perhaps most revered for his brilliant zombie film *Dellamorte Dellamore* (1994), gets a complimentary writeup for his early-career giallo *Stage Fright* (1987).

The writeup on Argento's *Sleepless* (2001) strikes me as (again, uncharacteristically) off the mark. While I view the film as Argento's return to form, Howarth sees it as a tired rehash of Argento's better, earlier films. Still these nitpickings are very minor in light of the fact that Italian genre film fans and scholars now have a two-volume English-language set of books covering everything giallo. Both books are filled with striking lurid poster art of many of the films, which complements the reviews with stunning marketing materials to stimulate readers' imaginations. Howarth was honored with a Rondo Award nomination for these texts, and I find no reason to disagree with voters that these works are essential reading for all fans and scholars of Italian genre cinema.

A Promising Start

S. T. Joshi

MICHAEL GRIFFIN. *The Lure of Devouring Light.* Introduction by John Langan. Petaluma, CA: Word Horde, 2016. 319 pp. ISBN 9781939905192. $16.99 tpb.

This book appears to be receiving high accolades from a cadre of Mr. Griffin's friends and supporters—an understandable bit of log-rolling for a first short story collection by an author who hopes to establish himself as a figure in contemporary weird fiction. I am not sure the accolades are entirely deserved, but I am convinced that Michael Griffin has the native talent to become a meritorious writer—far more so than the overrated blowhard

Scott Nicolay and certain other writers one could mention.

The chief quality that Griffin brings to his writing is deftness in prose. At its best, Griffin's prose is luminous, lapidary, and evocative. His gift for language is admirable, and his insight into human character is often penetrating and insightful. He does, of course, have some limitations. All too often, his prose—and, more pertinently, his conceptions and his skill at narration—are not at their best. He has particular trouble with punctuation. He knows of no punctuation aside from commas and periods, and even these he handles poorly; he is blissfully unaware of the value and efficacy of the semicolon, the colon, and the dash. As with so many of his contemporaries, he lapses into stylistic and grammatical infelicities (the misuse of "like" for "as" or "as if"; run-on sentences; even misspellings such as "hippy" for "hippie"). And, as has become drearily common with the small press, his publisher has not seen fit to clean up Griffin's work with the use of a skilled copy editor.

But Griffin's problems go farther than occasional clumsiness in prose. He is afflicted with that most dreaded of literary faults, pretentiousness—a fault of which a number of other writers of his circle (I am obliged to mention Laird Barron and Joseph S. Pulver, Sr. as among the worst culprits) are guilty. Pretentiousness exhibits itself in the very titles of Griffin's stories, whether it be the title story or such things as "Dreaming Awake in the Tree of the World" or "The Book of Shattered Mornings"; or in the ponderous quotations from an imaginary book in "The Jewel in the Eye" ("Nothing remains pristine. No wish is strong enough to preserve the smooth reflection of idealized self"). Pretentiousness is a sin and a crime because it creates the pretence of highbrow sophistication and profundity; it suggests an author preening himself and patting himself on the back for being clever and "literary." It is fundamentally dishonest and insincere.

Griffin is fatally addicted to scenarios that rely on mere bizarrerie to generate terror and wonder; he is a bit short on coherence and narrative finish. The title story tells of a famous cellist (who also happens to be a sexual predator) whose playing somehow summons a strange female figure, with the result that the cellist is burned up. No attempt is made to account for the presence of this figure; instead, we are simply treated to a succession of affected descriptions of avant-garde music. "Dreaming Awake in the Tree of the World" features another odd woman who has lured a young man into living in a tree by way of psychedelic mushrooms. That is the extent of the story.

"The Book of Shattered Mornings" is the first-person account of a man, apparently suffering serious injuries, finding a book that appears to contain episodes from his past life. It is a beautifully written story, but its overall thrust is not evident. "No Mask to Conceal Her Voice" is an impressionistic but rather confused and incoherent riff on Chambers's *The King in Yellow*.

One of the worst stories in the book—and one that painfully highlights Griffin's deficiencies—is "The Jewel in the Eye." Here the author has come up with a potentially powerful idea—the idea that certain people have the ability to fashion "shapers," or quasi-human dolls, out of their imaginations. A woman designs such a shaper in the form of her younger self, for her husband to have sex with. What could have been a gripping tale that probes issues of identity, fidelity, and so on is spoiled by windy pseudophilosophical discussions and irrelevant episodes.

Griffin has particular problems with longer narratives. There are two in this book, the novella "Far from Streets" and the short novel *The Black Vein Runs Deep*. "Far from Streets" begins compellingly, as a man named Dane builds a cabin in a remote plot of land in the forests of Oregon. His wife, Carolyn, is devoted to the city, and some of the more intense passages in the story deal with their sharp arguments over the relative values of city and country life. But the tale is peppered with all manner of episodes that have no relevance to the basic plot (assuming there even is a plot). Griffin makes much of the fact that Dane unearths a saucer-like stone with possible signs or writing on it. This object is brought in again at the end of the tale, but its significance is never clarified. There are numerous other elements that are not properly accounted for—and, more relevantly, that bear no clear relation to the city-country dichotomy that is at the heart of the tale. Perhaps Griffin, unwisely adopting one of the least admirable qualities of Robert Aickman, feels that he can simply throw in these elements to augment the strangeness of the narrative; but in fact he is doing the reader a disservice. Alert readers will want such elements to *mean something* in the overall narrative; when they fail to do so, there is an inevitable feeling of frustration and disappointment.

This problem is magnified in *The Black Vein Runs Deep,* which could have been a spectacular novel of underground terror. Here we are led to believe that there was a serious accident, killing twenty or more people, at a gold mine near the town of Kinosha, Oregon. Two people conducting a geological survey of the area, Adison Kye and Colman Quinn, find that the elderly owner of the mine, Lewin McAttree, seems to be hiding something. As they continue their investigation, the tension grows—until it is lamentably dissipated by long discussions between Adison and Colman about their personal lives (each is or has been involved in a failed marriage). This may all be in the interest of character portrayal, but its presentation in a big lump in the centre of the story cripples the pace of the narrative. Even when the story returns to the actual plot, grippingly describing the two protagonists' probing of the mine as they descend far into the bowels of the earth, Griffin fails to deliver. He engenders a scenario where some invisible creature or creatures create mayhem in the depths of the mine, but then seems to forget all about this vital matter to dwell on Adison leading Colman to some ill-defined wonderland. Toward the end we get a passage like this:

> New life coalesces, growing. Biology quivers with aspiration, yearns to challenge a patient, malicious universe. A foundry of one budding to infinity, emitting heat in its slow shift from embryonic potentiality to imminent ego-actor, awhirl with creative ambition and causative intent, soon to crack through the fragile shell of this tired Earth, shrug off ruptured shards, and like a chrysalis shed our obsoleted world.

Let it pass that the word "obsoleted" has not been used since the late seventeenth century; this is pretentiousness, pure and undiluted. It is all bombast and fustian, all sound and fury signifying nothing.

But it would be unfair to focus on the (sadly numerous) instances in this collection where the stories fail to deliver on their promises. When we turn to a story like "Diamond Dust," we are inclined to forgive Michael Griffin all the literary blunders he has made elsewhere. This story is a splendid example of what might be called industrial horror, envisioning some hideous fusion of humanity and steel. (The imagery is likely to have come from personal experience, as Griffin spent more than twenty years working in a steel factory.) In contrast to the incoherent passage above, consider this:

> Creatures barely human climb slippery hot from the melt pool, pass without stopping and slither over the brink. Each descends to an ordained position and slowly hardens in place. Bound together in an agonized realm of ash and steel, their relinquished dreams and forgotten pleasures form underpinnings of a new, transformed world.

Magnificent! There is no question that "Diamond Dust" is one of the more powerful weird tales written in this new millennium.

Other stories in the collection do not quite measure up to this one, but are nonetheless admirable. "Arches and Pillars" is a kind of stream-of-consciousness story of a man's ambiguous relationship with a man, featuring an effective atmosphere of unreality. "The Accident of Survival," written in a similarly free-flowing manner, tells of a man and his partner narrowly avoiding a crash with an oncoming truck—or have they in fact died in the crash?

Most short story collections are uneven, but Griffin's seems rather more uneven than the norm, ranging from the superb to the sadly mediocre. But there is enough good work here to hint at better things to come. Michael Griffin has by no means arrived; and if he can avoid believing in the encomiums of his cheerleaders (as Laird Barron has failed to do, to the point that his recent work is close to unreadable), and if he can grasp the need to make further improvements in all aspects of his writing, he will do more creditable work in the future.

Capsule Reviews

ROGER LUCKHURST. *Zombies: A Cultural History*. London: Reaktion Books, 2015. 224 pp. ISBN 9781780236698. £16.00 hc, £9.99 tpb.

Zombies: A Cultural History is the most comprehensive account to date of this relatively recent variety of monster. Luckhurst's book is unique in its coverage of the zombie's evolution before George Romero's iconic transformation of the creature in his 1968 film *Night of the Living Dead*. The first two chapters are devoted to analyzing the first two accounts of Haitian zombie folklore: Lafcadio Hearn's "The Country of Comers Back" and William Seabrook's "Dead Men Working in the Cane Fields." Both introduced wider audiences to the zombie, a figure that was more piteous than fearful, as it was someone deprived of free will by a sorcerer for the purposes of enslavement. Later chapters explore the creature's slow evolution in cinema and in pulp publications in the 1930s and 1940s, with one chapter devoted to Felicia Felix-Mentor, the allegedly "real" zombie described by folklorist Zora Neale Hurston in *Tell My Horse,* an account of her visit to Haiti. The concluding three chapters discuss representations of the creature after World War II, Romero's reimagining of the zombie trope, and its persistence in popular culture. [June Pulliam]

JOHN C. TIBBETTS. *The Gothic Worlds of Peter Straub.* Jefferson, NC: McFarland, 2016. x, 248 pp. ISBN 9781476664927. $35.00 tpb.

John C. Tibbetts, a professor of film and media studies at the University of Kansas, has emerged as a leading critic of weird fiction, if his scintillating book of essays and interviews, *The Gothic Imagination* (Palgrave Macmillan, 2011), is any gauge. He now directs his attention to a subject that has long fascinated him, Peter Straub, whose variegated array of short stories, novellas, and novels seems perfectly suited to Tibbetts's sophisticated analysis. The result is a splendidly illuminating study of this complex and at times opaque writer. Tibbetts focuses on the entirety of Straub's works, from the short stories in *Houses without Doors* (1990) and *Interior Darkness* (2007) to novels ranging from *Ghost Story* (1979) to *A Dark Matter* (2010). While studying Straub's forays into supernatural fiction, mystery fiction, Lovecraftian fiction, and his collaborations with Stephen King, Tibbetts draws upon several interviews he has conducted with Straub (the book concludes with a lengthy interview done in 2011 and updated in 2016). This book will immediately take its place as an essential guide to Straub's multifarious output. [S. T. Joshi]

Notes on Contributors

Michael J. Abolafia lives in New York City, where he studies English at Columbia University. His writing has appeared in *Sunlit*, *Supernatural Tales*, the *New York Daily News* online book blog, *Page Views*, and other venues. With David E. Schultz, he co-edited Park Barnitz's *The Book Of Jade: A Critical Edition* for Hippocampus Press. He is looking forward to assuming co-editorship (with Alex Houstoun) of *Dead Reckonings* in 2017.

Leigh Blackmore has written weird verse since age thirteen. He has lived in the Illawarra, New South Wales, Australia, for the last decade. He has edited *Terror Australis: Best Australian Horror* (1993) and *Midnight Echo* 5 (2011) and written *Spores from Sharnoth & Other Madnesses* (2008). A nominee for SFPA's Rhysling Award (Best Long Poem), Leigh is also a four-time Ditmar Award nominee. He is currently compiling his second collection of fantastic verse and writing a thriller novel.

Richard Bleiler is author of, among other things, *The Reference and Research Guide to Mystery and Detective Fiction* (Libraries Unlimited, 2004), coauthor of *Science Fiction: The Early Years* (Kent State University Press, 1990) and *Science Fiction: The Gernsback Years* (Kent State University Press, 1998), and editor of such works as *Supernatural Fiction Writers: Contemporary Fantasy and Horror* (Scribner/Macmillan, 2003). He most recently edited editions of Robert W. Cole's *The Struggle for Empire* and Samuel Barton's *The Battle of the Swash,* which were published as volume one in *Political Future Fiction: Speculative and Counter-Factual Politics in Edwardian Fiction* (Pickering & Chatto, 2013). He is also the Humanities Librarian at the Homer Babbidge Library at the University of Connecticut.

Jason V Brock is an award-winning writer, editor, filmmaker, composer, and artist, and has been widely published online, in comic books, magazines, and anthologies such as *Butcher Knives*

& *Body Counts, Disorders of Magnitude, Simulacrum and Other Possible Realities, Fungi, Weird Fiction Review, Fangoria,* and S. T. Joshi's *Black Wings* series. He was art director/managing editor for *Dark Discoveries* magazine, and currently has a biannual pro digest called [*NameL3ss*], which can be found on Twitter: @NamelessMag, and on the Interwebs at www.NamelessMag.com. Brock's films include the critically acclaimed documentaries *Charles Beaumont: The Life of Twilight Zone's Magic Man, The AckerMonster Chronicles!* (winner of the 2014 Rondo Hatton Award for Best Documentary), and *Image, Reflection, Shadow: Artists of the Fantastic.* He is the author of a short story collection and of the treatise *Disorders of Magnitude* (Rowman & Littlefield, 2015). Brock and his wife, Sunni, run Cycatrix Press, and have a technology consulting business. He loves his family of reptiles and amphibians, travel, and veganism.

The *Oxford Companion to English Literature* describes **Ramsey Campbell** as "Britain's most respected living horror writer." He has been given more awards than any other writer in the field, including the Grand Master Award of the World Horror Convention, the Lifetime Achievement Award of the Horror Writers Association, and the Living Legend Award of the International Horror Guild. Among his novels are *The Face That Must Die, Incarnate, Midnight Sun, The Count of Eleven, Silent Children, The Darkest Part of the Woods, The Overnight, Secret Story, The Grin of the Dark, Thieving Fear, Creatures of the Pool, The Seven Days of Cain, Ghosts Know, The Kind Folk,* and *Think Yourself Lucky.* Forthcoming is *Thirteen Days at Sunset Beach.* "The Last Revelation of Gla'aki" and "The Pretence" are novellas. His collections include *Waking Nightmares, Alone with the Horrors, Ghosts and Grisly Things, Told by the Dead, Just Behind You,* and *Holes for Faces,* and his nonfiction is collected as *Ramsey Campbell, Probably.* His novels *The Nameless* and *Pact of the Fathers* have been filmed in Spain. His regular columns appear in *Prism, Dead Reckonings,* and *Video Watchdog.* He is the President of the Society of Fantastic Films. Ramsey Campbell lives on Merseyside with his wife, Jenny. His pleasures include classical music, good food and wine, and whatever's in that pipe. His website is at www.ramseycampbell.com.

Born in Italy, **Simone Caroti** wanted another place, so he left. He moved to West Lafayette, Indiana, in 2002 to pursue a master's degree and a Ph.D. in comparative literature at Purdue University. While there, Simone taught Italian, English composition, literature, and business writing, and received his Ph.D. in 2009 with a dissertation on science fiction. In 2011, that dissertation became a book, *The Generation Starship in Science Fiction: A Critical History, 1934–2001* (McFarland), and a second followed in March 2015—*The Culture Series of Iain M. Banks: A Critical Introduction* (McFarland). In December 2010, Simone moved to Florida with his wife; she has a job at NASA, he's spaced, and they're happy. He taught prep writing, composition, literature, and science fiction at Brevard Community College; he now teaches fantasy and science fiction in the creative writing BFA. He is also a Senior Research Scientist at the Astrosociology Research Institute (ARI), an organization devoted to bringing the humanities and the social sciences into the debate on human colonization of outer space.

Chris Dallis has degrees in English and philosophy. He is a cinephile and bibliomaniac who loves discovering amazing, lesser-known films and books. Chris hopes one day to move to California and direct films from his own screenplays. Currently, his favorite types of films are Eurocrime flicks, Spaghetti Westerns, and exploitation horror films, and his all-time hero is Quentin Tarantino because the director is able to turn his love of bloody exploitation cinema into alarmingly entertaining, award-winning dramatic art.

Tony Fonseca is a librarian at Elms College in Massachusetts. He has coauthored three volumes of *Hooked on Horror* (with June Michele Pulliam), as well as *Read On . . . Horror,* and has contributed to *Icons of Horror and the Supernatural* and *Encyclopedia of the Vampire* (both edited by S. T. Joshi), and was a reviewer with *Necrofile*. He has published articles on gender-based reactions to horror and on vampire music, and on Ramsey Campbell, Dracula's *Daughter/Nadja,* and Robert Aickman. His study of Richard Matheson, coauthored with June Pulliam, is forthcoming from Rowman & Littlefield.

Greg Gbur is an associate professor of physics and optical science at the University of North Carolina at Charlotte, specializing in theoretical optics. He published his first book, *Mathematical Methods for Physics and Optical Science,* in 2011. Since 2007, he has been writing the blog Skulls in the Stars, where he shares his enthusiasm about a variety of topics including optics, the history of science, classic horror fiction, and the often surprising connections between them. Since early 2013, he has written seven introductions to John Blackburn's novels for Valancourt Books.

David Goudsward lives in Florida in the shadow of the Lake Worth Muck Monster, but was raised in the haunted woods of Haverhill, Massachusetts, hometown of Rob Zombie, axe murderess Hannah Duston, and a disturbingly large number of horror writers. He is the author of 14 books on various nonfiction topics, including *H. P. Lovecraft in the Merrimack Valley* and the forthcoming *H. P. Lovecraft in Florida*, both from Hippocampus Press. His next books, *Horror Guide to Northern New England* (Post Mortem Press) and *Sun, Sand, and Sea Serpents: A History of Florida Sea Monster Sightings* (McFarland Publishing) will be released in 2017.

S. T. Joshi is the author of such critical studies as *The Weird Tale* (1990), *H. P. Lovecraft: The Decline of the West* (1990), and *Unutterable Horror: A History of Supernatural Fiction* (2012). He has prepared corrected editions of H. P. Lovecraft's work for Arkham House and annotated editions of the weird tales of Lovecraft, Algernon Blackwood, Lord Dunsany, M. R. James, and Arthur Machen for Penguin Classics, as well as the anthology *American Supernatural Tales* (2007). His exhaustive biography, *H. P. Lovecraft: A Life* (1996), won the British Fantasy Award and the Bram Stoker Award from the Horror Writers Association; an unabridged and updated edition has appeared as *I Am Providence: The Life and Times of H. P. Lovecraft* (2010). He has also edited works by Ambrose Bierce, H. L. Mencken, and other writers, and has written on religion, politics, and race relations.

Alexander Lugo hails from the hallowed heights of northern

New Jersey, a source in itself of many piquant terrors and abnormalities. He has been an ardent reader and exponent of weird and speculative fiction for close to a decade and has written genre reviews for T. E. Grau's *The Cosmicomicon* and Justin Steele's *Arkham Digest* (not to mention a failed novel or three). Besides many obsessive readings of Lovecraft, McCarthy, Ligotti, and Miller, Lugo finds great joy in his many obsessive listenings to the music of Miles Davis, Pink Floyd, and Scott Walker, among many others. He is currently studying English at Cornell University.

At the tender age of eight, **June Pulliam** was permitted to stay up by herself and watch George Romero's *Night of the Living Dead.* She was so traumatized by the experience, that she now teaches courses on horror fiction at Louisiana State University. She is the author of *Monstrous Bodies: Feminine Power in Young Adult Horror Fiction,* as well as many articles on fantastic young adult fiction, Roald Dahl, and zombie studies. Additionally, Pulliam has authored (with Anthony Fonseca) three volumes of *Hooked on Horror, Read On . . . Horror,* and *The Encyclopedia of the Zombie: The Walking Dead in Popular Culture and Myth.* Her books *Richard Matheson: Stories, Scripts, Novels, and* Twilight Zone *Episodes* and *The Ghost in Legend and Popular Culture* are forthcoming from Rowman & Littlefield and ABC-CLIO.

Darrell Schweitzer is a fantasy and horror novelist and short-story writer, author of *The Mask of the Sorcerer, The Shattered Goddess,* and *The White Isle,* and roughly 300 published stories. He is a four-time World Fantasy Award nominee and one-time winner, as co-editor of *Weird Tales,* a position he held for nineteen years. His criticism, reviews, and essays have appeared in the *Philadelphia Inquirer,* the *Washington Post, Publishers Weekly,* the *New York Review of Science Fiction, Lovecraft Studies,* and elsewhere. He has published books on Lord Dunsany and H. P. Lovecraft and edited such critical symposia as *The Thomas Ligotti Reader, The Robert E. Howard Reader,* and *Discovering H. P. Lovecraft.* His most recent book is *Speaking of the Fantastic III,* a book of interviews.

Index to *Dead Reckonings* 11–20

Conspectus of issues:

I. Index of Contributors

II. Index of Authors Reviewed

III. Index of Titles Reviewed

DEAD RECKONINGS is published by Hippocampus Press, P.O. Box 641, New York, NY 10156 (www.hippocampuspress.com). Copyright © 2016 by Hippocampus Press. Cover art by Jason C. Eckhardt. Cover design by Barbara Briggs Silbert. Hippocampus Press logo by Anastasia Damianakos. Orders and subscriptions should be sent to Hippocampus Press. Contact Alex Houstoun at ahoustoun@gmail.com before submitting a publication for review.

ISSN 1935-6110

www.ingramcontent.com/pod-product-compliance
Lightning Source LLC
Chambersburg PA
CBHW071126090426
42736CB00012B/2022